THE
PASSION
TRANSLATION

THE PASSIONATE LIFE BIBLE STUDY SERIES

12-LESSON STUDY GUIDE

THE BOOK OF
GENESIS

PART TWO
Chapters 12–50

firstfruits

tPt

BroadStreet
PUBLISHING

BroadStreet Publishing® Group, LLC
Savage, Minnesota, USA
BroadStreetPublishing.com

TPT The Book of Genesis – Part 2: 12-Lesson Study Guide
Copyright © 2022 BroadStreet Publishing Group

978-1-4245-6411-8 (softcover)
978-1-4245-6412-5 (e-book)

Stock or custom editions of BroadStreet Publishing titles may be purchased in bulk for educational, business, ministry, fundraising, or sales promotional use. For information, please email orders@broadstreetpublishing.com.

General editor: Brian Simmons
Managing editor: William D. Watkins
Writer: William D. Watkins

Design and typesetting | garborgdesign.com

Printed in the United States of America

22 23 24 25 26 5 4 3 2 1

Contents

From God's Heart to Yours

"God is love," says the apostle John, and "Everyone who loves is fathered by God and experiences an intimate knowledge of him" (1 John 4:7). The life of a Christ-follower is, at its core, a life of love—God's love of us, our love of him, and our love of others and ourselves because of God's love for us.

And this divine love is reliable, trustworthy, unconditional, other-centered, majestic, forgiving, redemptive, patient, kind, and more precious than anything else we can ever receive or give. It characterizes each person of the Trinity—Father, Son, and Holy Spirit—and so is as unlimited as they are. They love one another with this eternal love, and they reach beyond themselves to us, created in their image with this love.

How do we know such incredible truths? Through the primary source of all else we know about the one God—his Word, the Bible. Of course, God reveals who he is through other sources as well, such as the natural world, miracles, our inner life, our relationships (especially with him), those who minister on his behalf, and those who proclaim him to us and others. But the fullest and most comprehensive revelation we have of God and from him is what he has given us in the thirty-nine books of the Hebrew Scriptures (the Old Testament) and the twenty-seven books of the Christian Scriptures (the New Testament). Together, these sixty-six books present a compelling and telling portrait of God and his dealings with us.

It is these Scriptures that *The Passionate Life Bible Study Series* is all about. Through these study guides, we—the editors and writers of this series—seek to provide you with a unique and welcoming opportunity to delve more deeply into God's precious Word, encountering there his loving heart for you and all the others he loves. God wants you to know him more deeply, to love him more devoutly, and to share his heart with others more frequently and freely. To accomplish this, we have based this study guide series on The Passion Translation of the Bible, which strives to "unlock the passion of [God's] heart." It is "a heart-level translation, from the passion of God's heart to the passion of your heart," created to "kindle in you a burning desire for him and his heart, while impacting the church for years to come."[1]

In each study guide, you will find an introduction to the Bible book it covers. There you will gain information about that Bible book's authorship, date of composition, first recipients, setting, purpose, central message, and key themes. Each lesson following the introduction will take a portion of that Bible book and walk you through it so you will learn its content better while experiencing and applying God's heart for your own life and encountering ways you can share his heart with others. Along the way, you will come across a number of features we have created that provide opportunities for more life application and growth in biblical understanding:

 ## Experience God's Heart

This feature focuses questions on personal application. It will help you live out God's Word, to bring the Bible into your world in fresh, exciting, and relevant ways.

 ## Share God's Heart

This feature will help you grow in your ability to share with other people what you learn and apply in a given lesson. It provides guidance on how the lesson relates to growing closer to others, to enriching your fellowship with others. It also points the way to enabling you to better listen to the stories of others so you can bridge the biblical story with their stories.

The Backstory

This feature provides ancient historical and cultural background that illuminates Bible passages and teachings. It deals with then-pertinent religious groups, communities, leaders, disputes, business trades, travel routes, customs, nations, political factions, ancient measurements and currency...in short, anything historical or cultural that will help you better understand what Scripture says and means. You may also find maps and charts that will help you reimagine these groups, places, and activities. Finally, in this feature you will find references to additional Bible texts that will further illuminate the Scripture you are studying.

 Word Wealth

This feature provides definitions and other illuminating information about key terms, names, and concepts, and how different ancient languages have influenced the biblical text. It also provides insight into the different literary forms in the Bible, such as prophecy, poetry, narrative history, parables, and letters, and how knowing the form of a text can help you better interpret and apply it. Finally, this feature highlights the most significant passages in a Bible book. You may be encouraged to memorize these verses or keep them before you in some way so you can actively hide God's Word in your heart.

 Digging Deeper

This feature explains the theological significance of a text or the controversial issues that arise and mentions resources you can use to help you arrive at your own conclusions. Another way to dig deeper into the Word is by looking into the life of a biblical character or another person from church history, showing how that man or woman incarnated a biblical truth or passage. For instance, Jonathan Edwards was well known for his missions work among native American Indians and for his intellectual prowess in articulating the Christian faith; Florence Nightingale for the reforms she brought about in healthcare; Irenaeus for his fight against heresy; Billy Graham for his work in evangelism; Moses for the strength God gave him to lead the Hebrews and receive and communicate the law; Deborah for her work as a judge in Israel. This feature introduces to you figures from the past who model what it looks like to experience God's heart and share his heart with others.

The Extra Mile

While The Passion Translation's notes are extensive, sometimes students of Scripture like to explore more on their own. In this feature, we provide you with opportunities to glean more information from a Bible dictionary, a Bible encyclopedia, a reliable Bible online tool, another ancient text, and the like. Here you will learn how you can go the extra mile on a Bible lesson. And not just in study either. Reflection, prayer, discussion, and applying a passage in new ways provide even more opportunities to go the extra mile. Here you will find questions to answer and applications to make that will require more time and energy from you—if and when you have them to give.

As you can see above, each of these features has a corresponding icon so you can quickly and easily identify them.

You will find other helps and guidance through the lessons of these study guides, including thoughtful questions, application suggestions, and spaces for you to record your own reflections, answers, and action steps. Of course, you can also write in your own journal, notebook, computer, or other resource, but we have provided you with space for your convenience.

Also, each lesson will direct you into the introductory material and numerous notes provided in The Passion Translation. There each Bible book contains a number of aids supplied to help you better grasp God's words and his incredible love, power, knowledge, plans, and so much more. We want you to get the most out of your Bible study, especially using it to draw you closer to the One who loves you most.

Finally, at the end of each lesson you'll find a section called "Talking It Out." This contains questions and exercises for application that you can share, answer, and apply with your spouse, a friend, a coworker, a Bible study group, or any other individuals or groups who would like to walk with you through this material. As Christians, we gather together to serve, study, worship, sing, evangelize, and a host of other activities. We grow together, not just on our own. This section will give you ample opportunities to engage others with the content of each lesson so you can work it out in community.

We offer all of this to support you in becoming an even more faithful and loving disciple of Jesus Christ. A disciple in the ancient world was a student of her teacher, a follower of his master. Students study and followers follow. Jesus' disciples are to sit at his feet and listen and learn and then do what he tells them and shows them to do. We have created *The Passionate Life Bible Study Series* to help you do what a disciple of Jesus is called to do.

So go.

Read God's words.

Hear what he has to say in them and through them.

Meditate on them.

Hide them in your heart.

Display their truths in your life.

Share their truths with others.

Let them ignite Jesus' passion and light in all you say and do.

Use them to help you fulfill what Jesus called his disciples to do: "Now wherever you go, make disciples of all nations, baptizing them in the name of the Father, the Son, and the Holy Spirit. And teach them to faithfully follow all that I have commanded you. And never forget that I am with you every day, even to the completion of this age" (Matthew 28:19–20).

And through all of this, let Jesus' love nourish your heart and allow that love to overflow into your relationships with others (John 15:9–13). For it was for love that Jesus came, served, died, rose from the dead, and ascended into heaven. This love he gives us. And this love he wants us to pass along to others.

Why I Love the Patriarchs

Abraham, Isaac, Jacob, Joseph. The true stories of these four men captivate and fascinate me. There's something about real-life stories that hold our attention. They have the starring roles in the dramatic history of Israel. God's gracious blessing flowing through them now comes to every believer today. Let's look at these four champions of faith.

To me, the life of Abraham is a beautiful picture of the life of faith. He left everything behind to follow the divine voice. He and his barren wife, Sarah, were blessed with a miracle child. That tells me that faith is what births a miracle. Abraham was an intercessor, one who fought for his family. He ultimately made his beloved son an offering to God, believing that God would raise his son from the dead (Hebrews 11:19). The life-lesson of Abraham was to live by faith. I love the story of Abraham because he is the father of faith, the father of *my* faith.

The life of Isaac is a great example to me of living in the inheritance of God. Isaac is marked by the blessings of his father. He inherited that immense blessing of God as a son of favor. Isaac dug wells and uncovered the wells of his father. In a sense, Isaac's story is our story, for we, too, have inherited all things as a son or daughter of God (1 Corinthians 3:21). I love the story of Isaac because he is the patriarch of *my* inheritance in Christ.

The life of Jacob—a riveting story of how God grips the heart of a trickster and transforms him into a prince. Jacob received the coveted blessing, or shall we say, Jacob *stole* that blessing from his brother. Yet God favored Jacob throughout his life. He wrestled with his brother, he wrestled with Laban, and he wrestled with God. There is hope for me and for you, even if, for a season, we fall into personal struggles with our destiny. I love the story of Jacob because he became Israel, God's prince.

The life of Joseph is a story of going from riches to rags to riches. The up-and-down path of Joseph's life is a wonderful picture of how God works through everything in our life to bring us to the place of honor. Joseph is an example to me of how important forgiveness is; he forgave the ones who hurt him most. Joseph realized that it was his brothers' betrayal that led him to the throne. Joseph was a dreamer and a prophet. His excellent character survived the pit and the prison until the day came when he was promoted to the palace. I love the story of Joseph because I see in his life the lessons I need to live a pure and holy life before God.

Because Genesis is so foundational to the rest of history, we decided to cover it in two study guides. The first one (Part 1) covers the first eleven chapters of Genesis, from creation to the confusion of human languages during the construction of the tower of Babel. The second study guide (Part 2), which is this one, works through the rest of Genesis, from God's choice of Abraham to the last days of Jacob and Joseph—the era of the patriarchs. I hope you will take the next several weeks to pour through the pages of this second part of the Genesis Bible study guides. I know you'll love reading through these lessons. Let God speak to you and reveal to you the life-lessons of the patriarchs!

Brian Simmons
General Editor

LESSON 1

Abram, Sarai, and Blessings for All

(11:10–13:18)

The human race starts with a human pair. They have children, their adult children have children, and on the process goes until divine judgment must fall on the corruption that has overtaken the race. Through the global judgment of floodwaters, one man's family is saved. Through them, the repopulation of the earth begins and flourishes until their descendants plan to steal dominion from God and advance their own plans and glory. This, too, brings judgment. Human language is confused and divided, and the peoples disperse across the earth, finally in (reluctant?) obedience to God.

All the while, God is at work, fulfilling a prophecy he directed to Satan in Eden: "I will place great hostility between you and the woman, and between her seed and yours. He will crush your head as you crush his heel" (Genesis 3:15). Eve's progenies have so far survived, even if barely through the flood. After the flood, they have finally dispersed throughout Europe, northern and eastern Africa, Russia, Assyria, Persia, and Arabia. They are filling the earth, subduing it, and flourishing in it. But what about the seed to come? Through whom will this predicted seed be realized?

The latter part of Genesis 11 and the opening of chapter 12 provide the answer. God's plan will not be stopped. He will ensure that the seed comes through another couple. Just as the human race began with one married pair, so the redeemed among the human race will also start with one human pair.

The Line of Shem

Just as we choose according to our will, God chooses according to his. And among Noah's three sons, God chose Shem's line through which to bring the one who would conquer Satan and establish salvation for all who would put their trust in him (Luke 3:23, 36; 10:17–20; Colossians 2:13–16).

Genesis 11:10–26 is Book 5, the start of which contains the fifth use of the *toledot* formula in Genesis: "These are the descendants [*toledot*] of Shem." (The previous four books are 2:4–4:26, 5:1–6:8, 6:9–9:29, and 10:1–11:9, each a family history.[2]) In this list, some persons in Shem's line are repeated from Genesis 10 while others appear for the first time. The repeated names are Arphaxad (11:10; 10:22), Shelah (11:12; 10:24), Eber (11:14; 10:21, 24–25), and Peleg (11:16; 10:25–26). But even with these names, new information is supplied. The new names on the list are Reu (11:18), Serug (11:20), Nahor (Abram's grandfather, v. 22), Terah (v. 24), Abram (v. 26), Nahor (Abram's brother, v. 26), and Haran (v. 26).

- For each of the following individuals, record what the text says about their age when they had one of their sons, then how much longer they lived afterward, and then add the figures together to learn how long each one lived.

Shem (10:10–11): Age when son was born _____ ; number of years lived afterward _____ ; total number of years lived _____ .

Arphaxad (vv. 12–13): Age when son was born _____ ; number of years lived afterward _____ ; total number of years lived _____ .

Shelah (vv. 14–15): Age when son was born _____ ; number of years lived afterward _____ ; total number of years lived _____ .

Eber (vv. 16–17): Age when son was born _____ ; number of years lived afterward _____ ; total number of years lived _____ .

Peleg (vv. 18–19): Age when son was born _____ ; number of years lived afterward _____ ; total number of years lived _____ .

Reu (vv. 20–21): Age when son was born _____ ; number of years lived afterward _____ ; total number of years lived _____ .

Serug (vv. 22–23): Age when son was born _____ ; number of years lived afterward _____ ; total number of years lived _____ .

Nahor (vv. 24–25): Age when son was born _____ ; number of years lived afterward _____ ; total number of years lived _____ .

Terah (vv. 26, 32): Three sons at age _____ ; total number of years lived _____ .

- *What did you notice about the lifespans of these individuals? How do their lifespans differ from those human beings who lived before the great flood (see*

Genesis 5)? How does the lifespan of the post-flood individuals differ from Noah's (9:29)?

• *Relate your above answers to what God said he would do in 6:3. Did he work toward his intended age-restraint goal for humanity? Why do you suppose God took several generations to work out his plan?*

• *In Genesis 5, there's a short recurring phrase used to indicate the end of life that doesn't appear in chapter 11 until verse 28. What is it? What do you think is the significance of the almost total absence of this phrase in chapter 11?*

Although we know very little about Reu, Serug, and Nahor (Abram's grandfather), the physician and early church historian Luke found them important enough to mention them in his genealogy of Jesus (Luke 3:34–35).

- You may at times feel unimportant, but from God's vantage point, your life matters. Take some time now to let that truth sink in. We don't know what our true significance will be in the outworking of God's plan, but he knows, and he will never forget our service to him, and he will use it far beyond what we can ever imagine.

From Terah to Abram

In Book 4, Shem's genealogy ends with Joktan and those he fathered (Genesis 10:26–29). Book 5, however, ends Shem's line with Terah, the names of his three sons, and nothing about the length of his lifespan and death (11:26). Terah's line of descendants is left open, and among his sons is Abram, the first patriarch of the faith, the one with whom God will establish an everlasting covenant of blessing for all of humanity.

Book 6 (11:27–25:11) opens with a link back to the end of Book 5, focusing on Terah and his descendants.

- *Read 11:24–32. Jot down what you learn specifically about Terah. Also consult TPT's study notes on these verses.*

- *Now go back through the same section of Scripture and write what you find out about his sons Haran and Nahor. The study notes will offer some information too.*

- *Finally, read through these verses again but this time focusing on Abram. What do you learn about him? Be sure to consult the study notes as well.*

Abram and God's Promised Blessing

Abram (later renamed Abraham) becomes the first patriarch of Israel. With him begins what scholars refer to as "the patriarchal age." Along with Abram, the other patriarchs are Isaac and Jacob, all of whom appear in Genesis. Bible scholar Merrill Unger states: "Abraham was born c. 2161 b.c. and entered Canaan 2086 b.c. The patriarchal period would extend in this case from 2086 to 1871 b.c."[3]

Terah, Abram's father, lived with his family in "the Chaldean city of Ur" (Genesis 11:31). Ancient Ur was in southern Babylonia about 150 miles from the head of the Persian Gulf. It "had one of the most advanced cultures in the world." Archaeological evidence from the site includes "gold daggers and cups [that] witness the wealth of the [city's] culture."[4] Other artifacts include "jewelry and art treasures of unbelievable beauty, particularly gorgeous head attire, personal jewels,...musical instruments and other beautifully crafted objects...Archaeology has revealed that in Abraham's day Ur was a great and prosperous city, with perhaps 360,000 people living in the city and its suburbs."[5] According to Bible scholar Gleason Archer, "The average middle-class citizens lived in well-appointed houses containing from ten to twenty rooms. Schools were maintained for the education of the young, for schoolboy tablets have been discovered which attest their training in reading, writing, arithmetic, and religion."[6]

The sacred center of Ur included a ziggurat and a number of other buildings that were erected for the worship of the moon god, Nannar, and his consort, Ningal.[7] The ziggurat was "built as a series of stepped platforms with the house of the god on top. Its structure probably resembled the tower of Babel. The ziggurat is 200 feet long, 100 feet across, and 250–300 feet high."[8]

When Terah was in Ur with his family, Ur's king was Ur-Nammu, and he's the one responsible for the ziggurat built there. On a "ten-by-five-foot stela" erected by this king are words that give a polytheistic interpretation of what Genesis 11 records about the tower of Babel: "The erection of this tower highly offended all the gods. In a night they threw down what man had built and impeded their progress. They were scattered abroad and their speech was strange."[9] Ur was a city committed to idolatry, and it modeled itself after the failed city of Babel.

It was while Abram was here, in Ur, that Yahweh came to him with a command and promises of blessing (Genesis 15:7; Nehemiah 9:7; Acts 7:2–3).

- *Were Terah and his family influenced by Ur's worship of false gods (Joshua 24:2)?*

- *What are some ways that your surrounding culture tries to influence your faith beliefs and practices?*

- *While Abram was still in the midst of a pagan city and with a family who lived according to its ways, what did Yahweh command him to do (Genesis 12:1)?*

- *What did Yahweh promise that he would do for Abram in return (vv. 2–3)?*

- *How many times is some form of the word "bless" used in this portion of Scripture, and who is to be blessed?*

๗ WORD WEALTH

The verb "to bless" (*barak*) in the Bible occurs about 330 times. Its first occurrence is in Genesis 1:22 in reference to sea and sky creatures. It's used again in 1:28 to refer to God's promise upon humanity. Other early uses of the word are in 5:2 when it is used to describe the generations of Adam and Eve after their expulsion from Eden and in 9:1 when God blesses Noah and his family after the great flood. Its next occurrence is in 12:2–3 when God says he will bless Abram, his descendants, and even all the world's nations—and this even after Babel and the confusion of human language.

As we said in Lesson 1 of part 1 of the Genesis Bible study guide, *to bless* means to "'empower for abundant living in every sphere of life.' This abundant-life empowerment flows from a vibrant relationship with God."[10] Blessing is not automatic, nor is it earned. God is the giver of blessing, and we typically receive it from him when we commit ourselves to him and live our lives in relationship with him. As one Bible resource on biblical words points out: "The covenant promise [first made to Abraham] called the nations to seek the 'blessing' (cf. Isa. 2:2–4), but made it plain that the initiative in blessing rests with God, and that Abraham and his seed were the instruments of it."[11]

Up to this point in his life, Abram likely didn't know Yahweh. He lived in a city of idols. And yet God selected him to bless and through him to bless others. God's choice to bless is completely up to him.

- *Did Abram obey Yahweh (Genesis 12:4)? How old was he at the time?*

- *Imagine yourself in this situation. You have lived in an unbelieving city with all of its influences for three quarters of a century. You received your education there, worked there, and, in some ways, flourished there. And then the God you have not worshiped comes to you, commands you to leave your old life behind, and promises to bless you and all other peoples through you. What hindrances do you think you would face in even believing that such an encounter was real? And assuming you believed it was, how do you imagine you would have responded to God's call on your life?*

Abram, along with his father and brothers and their wives, left Ur and traveled about two hundred miles north to another Babylonian city called Haran. Haran was in what we know today as northern Iraq. "The city was on the busy caravan road connecting with Nineveh, Asshur, and Babylon in Mesopotamia, and with

Damascus, Tyre, and Egyptian cities" in the west and south.[12] Haran was also a center for the worship of the moon god. Abram stayed there with his family until his father died (Genesis 11:31–32; 12:4).

- *After his father's death, what did Abram do, and who went with him (12:4–5)?*

- *Once Abram arrived in Canaan, what did he do (vv. 6–9)?*

- *What did Yahweh tell him there, and how did Abram respond?*

- With the mention of the names of a few places in Canaan and the statement in 12:9 that Abram also journeyed "by stages through the southern desert region" of the land, Moses affirms that Abram traveled the extent of Canaan, taking in the land that Yahweh promised would one day be his. Drawing from TPT's study notes for 12:6–9, record below what you find about the places named:

Shechem (v. 6):

Tree of Moreh (v. 6):

Bethel (v. 8):

Ai (v. 8):

Southern desert region (v. 9):

❤ EXPERIENCE GOD'S HEART

- *Have you ever, under God's direction, traveled from one place to another, moved from one job to another, left one belief system for a different one, or made any other significant change in your life? Describe how God came to you, what he told you, and what you did. How did this change turn out for you and other people you influence?*

- *What did you learn about obeying God through this life change?*

Abram in Egypt

While Abram was in Canaan surveying the land God had promised to give to his descendants, "a severe famine struck the land of Canaan, forcing Abram to travel down to Egypt and live there as a foreigner" (12:7, 10). J. Barton Payne puts the date of this journey around 2091 BCE.[13]

- *To prepare for their entrance into Egypt, Abram faced a moral dilemma that would impact him and Sarai. What was this dilemma, and how did Abram choose to deal with it (12:11–13; see also 20:12 and TPT note 'a' for 12:13)?*

- *Had Abram correctly understood the situation he and his wife would face (12:14–16; also check out note 'c' in TPT for v. 16)? Support your answer.*

- By giving up Sarai, what was Abram risking even while saving both of their lives (vv. 2–3)?

- How did Yahweh respond to what Pharaoh did (v. 17)?

- What was Pharaoh's response to Abram as a consequence of God's judgment (vv. 18–20)?

- Between Abram and Pharaoh, who would you say acted more morally? Provide support for your answer.

 DIGGING DEEPER

God had promised Abram blessing upon him and his descendants, even though he and Sarai were childless at the time (15:2). Abram had accepted by faith what God told him. He even moved to a new land at God's direction. But when he had to go to Egypt, Abram chose deception over faith. And rather than becoming a blessing to Egypt (12:3), he brought judgment. Yes, he became rich but at the Egyptians' expense and under false pretenses. In fact, as Allen Ross explains, Abram's accumulated wealth "could have diverted him from retaining Sarai, the one person who was needed for fulfilling the promise. Moreover, it is generally assumed that Hagar was acquired during this Egyptian stay. In 'giving away' his wife, Sarai, Abram may have acquired Hagar, who later became his slave-wife (16:1–2)."[14] While Abram's deception worked in the short term, it displayed his lack of faith in God to protect him and his wife and thereby to keep fulfilling the divine promises made to them. It also set up a situation that would later further threaten God's way of fulfilling his promises to Abram.

- *Have you ever relied on what you knew was wrong in order to achieve what you believed was good or right? If so, how did that work out for you and for those around you?*

- *Is it ever morally right to do the immoral? Explain your answer.*

♥ SHARE GOD'S HEART

Actions confirm what we believe to be true and right. If we say truth-telling is right but then tell a lie, we undermine what we claim is good. If we say that loving others involves caring for their needs and then do nothing to care for the needs of others, we contradict our words by our refusal to help. Belief joined by action is what Scripture reveals to be a living, authentic faith (James 2:14–26). Love requires demonstration, as Jesus said, "Love each other just as much as I have loved you. For when you demonstrate the same love I have for you by loving one another, everyone will know that you're my true followers" (John 13:34–35). Love in word only is not Christian love, and it will not draw other people to Jesus.

* *Sharing our faith with others in words is good, but doing that in action is even better, and it confirms and supports what we say. Who can you show what's right and true by your actions this week? Try doing the right and the good without words, then record below how your actions are received.*

Family Separation

After their expulsion from Egypt, Abram, Sarai, Lot, and all their families, slaves, and possessions "returned to the southern desert region" of Canaan (Genesis 13:1).

- *What quandary did Abram and Lot face back in Canaan (13:2–7)?*

- *How did they resolve their family problem (vv. 8–12)?*

- *What does the writer point out as an issue in the area where Lot chose to settle (v. 13)?*

- *When you have faced conflicts in your family, did you ever have to split up to maintain at least a semblance of civility? What are some compromises you have had to make? How have they worked out?*

- *After Lot left Abram, Yahweh once again spoke to Abram. What did Yahweh tell him (vv. 14–17)? Did God's words reinforce what he had promised Abram in chapter 12? How so?*

- *What was Abram's response to God's revelation (13:18)?*

Talking It Out

1. You may be young, middle age, or in your twilight years. God didn't call upon Abram for a special task until he was around seventy-five years old and Sarai was sixty-five. Much later in Israel's history, God first spoke to Samuel when he was still a young boy and then moved him into the role of a prophet later in his life (1 Samuel 3). What do these events reveal about God and his regard for our physical age?

2. Abram obeyed Yahweh by faith when he left Haran to
   follow God's call, but Abram did not always make morally
   right decisions. Like Abram, we can be people of faith and
   yet sometimes behave immorally. What does this reveal
   about us? How does this link us back to Adam and Eve in
   Genesis 3 and our need for the fullness of redemption?[15]

3. Abram was a man of worship. When Yahweh appeared
   to him, Abram typically built an altar to Yahweh and
   worshiped him (Genesis 12:7–8; 13:4, 18). Why do you think
   that God's presence and revelation warranted worship? Why
   do you worship God?

LESSON 2

Rescue, Blessing, and Covenant

(14:1-16:16)

The first war that Scripture records is the one described in Genesis 14. It's provoked by years of oppression that led to revolt (14:3–4). Four tyrant kings from out of the east "suppress a revolt by five kings in the Dead Sea area."[16]

> The names of the four eastern kings are listed in alphabetical order [in the Hebrew], though Kedorlaomer is their leader [see v. 1]...Their names suggest a very wide area from the Black Sea to the Persian Gulf, the whole Mesopotamian Valley, all of what later is Babylon and Asher. One explicitly comes from Elam (part of modern Iraq) and another from Shinar (modern Iraq). The other two are probably from Turkey.[17]

These four kings led their armies against five rebellious kings and their forces in southern Canaan (vv. 2–4). On their way, the four eastern kings conquered and plundered a number of places and peoples before arriving to array for battle against the five southern kings (vv. 5–7).

- *What happened when the four tyrannical eastern kings finally went to battle against the five rebellious kings (vv. 8–12)?*

- *How did Abram receive word about Lot's captivity (v. 13)?*

- *Where was Abram at this point in time (v. 13; cf. 13:18)?*

- *What was Abram's response when he heard about Lot's situation (14:14)?*

Abram's pursuit of the four kings with his much smaller force went "as far north as Dan" (v. 14). Dan was a city "at the southern foot of Mount Hermon," which was at the most northern end of the promised land (Judges 20:1; 1 Samuel 3:20).[18]

- *What strategy did Abram use against the four kings, and how effective was it (Genesis 14:15–16)?*

By chasing the invaders "north of Damascus" and recovering all their spoils, Abram, in effect, pushed them out of the promised land and sent them on their way empty-handed. His was a complete victory.

The Blessing of Melchizedek

After his victory, Abram traveled south again. When he reached "the valley of Shaveh (known as the King's Valley)" (14:17), which was near Jerusalem, he was met by a gentile priest named Melchizedek (v. 18).

- *Read verse 18 and TPT notes 'd' and 'e.' What did you learn about this king-priest?*

• *What did Melchizedek bring to give to Abram (v. 18)?*

• *What did this king-priest say to Abram (vv. 19–20)?*

• *To whom did Melchizedek give the credit for Abram's military victory?*

• *What did Abram give to this king-priest as a response to his blessing (v. 20)?*

God had promised Abram that through him the nations would be blessed (12:2–3). However, through Melchizedek, a gentile king-priest, one of the nations blessed Abram. Blessers bless, and the blessed pass along blessings.

❤ SHARE GOD'S HEART

• *When was the last time you blessed someone who has blessed you? How had they blessed you, and what did you eventually do to bless them?*

• *If for some time you haven't blessed someone who has blessed you, commit to remedying that situation very soon. Whom can you bless? What will you do and when? After you follow through, record here what happened.*

🔟 WORD WEALTH

Genesis 14:18 describes Melchizedek as "a priest of the Most High God and the king of Salem." The city-state of Salem was "the name of ancient Jerusalem."[19] *Salem* was the Canaanite term for "peace." It "would later give rise to the very meaningful Hebrew greeting *Shalom*," and "Salem would later contribute its five letters to form the last part of the name Jerusalem—'the foundation of peace.'"[20]

Furthermore, Melchizedek referred to God as "God Most High" (v. 19), *El Elyon.* Don Richardson explains:

> Both *El* and *Elyon* were Canaanite names for Yahweh Himself. *El* occurs frequently in ancient Ugaritic texts. This Canaanite name *El* even worked its way into the Hebrew language of Abram's descendants in such words as Beth*el*—"the house of God," *El Shaddai*—"God Almighty," and *Elohim*—"God" (a pluralized form of *El* which nevertheless retains a mysteriously singular meaning).
>
> *Elyon* likewise shows up as a name for God in ancient texts written in Phoenician—a later branch of Melchizedek's old Canaanite language. And even the compound form *El Elyon* appears in an ancient Aramaic inscription found recently in Syria. Compounded together, the two terms *El* and *Elyon* mean something like "the most God God," or "the God who is really God." Translators usually render it, "God most High."[21]

What Melchizedek apparently knew about God from general revelation (the divine unveiling through creation available to everyone) matched at least some of what Abram knew through special revelation (the divine unveiling through more personal means, such as the spoken word). Melchizedek was faithful to what he knew about God, and he honored Abram for acting faithfully to what he knew about that same God.

THE EXTRA MILE

The writer of Hebrews draws from Psalm 110:4 and Genesis 14 to make his case that Jesus Christ is the greatest King-Priest according to the order of the king-priest Melchizedek (Hebrews 5:1–10; 7:1–28). Read through these passages from Hebrews to glean what they reveal about Jesus' everlasting priesthood and how it's connected to Melchizedek, the king and priest of ancient Salem. You may also want to use TPT's Bible study guide *The Book of Hebrews: Living Faith*, especially Lesson 6.

When the king-priest Melchizedek greets Abram, he gives him something. In contrast, when the king of Sodom approached Abram, the king said to him, "give me" (Genesis 14:21). One king gave; the other king wanted.

· *Was the king of Sodom one of the victors in the war of the kings or one of those who suffered defeat (vv. 10–12)?*

· *What did the king of Sodom want from Abram (v. 21)?*

- As a defeated king who benefited from Abram's military victory, do you think the king of Sodom deserved to demand anything from Abram? Support your answer.

- What was Abram's response to the king's demand (vv. 22–24)?

God's Covenant with Abram

Sometime after Abram's return from victory and meeting with Melchizedek and the king of Sodom, Yahweh came to Abram in a vision (15:1). The Hebrew word translated "vision" here is rarely used in Scripture. "Second- and third-millennium Akkadian texts show that visions were a recognized and very ancient mode of revelation."[22]

- In this vision, what does Yahweh initially tell Abram (15:1)?

- *Abram responds to Yahweh with a complaint (vv. 2–3). What is it?*

- *What is Yahweh's answer to Abram (vv. 4–5)?*

- *How does Abram respond, and what is Yahweh's sign of approval (v. 6)?*

- *The apostle Paul draws from this experience in Abram's life to help explain what it means to receive righteousness from God. Look up Romans 4 and read through it. Write down what you learn about this kind of righteousness.*

- After reaffirming that Abram would have an heir from his own loins, Yahweh restated his promise to Abram regarding the land his heirs would possess. Read through the exchange between Yahweh and Abram on this matter recorded in Genesis 15:7–21.

What did Yahweh promise Abram (v. 7)?

What assurance did Abram need (v. 8)?

How did Yahweh supply that assurance (vv. 9–21)?

God let Abram know that the route of possessing the promised land would go through a foreign land in which his descendants would be "enslaved and mistreated for four hundred years" (v. 13). History would record that this foreign land was Egypt, and through the exodus, God delivered Abram's descendants, eventually bringing them into the promised land and using them to judge the people there for their great sins. Abram would witness none of this, but his heirs needed to know about it so they would be prepared for what was to come.

🔟 WORD WEALTH

"On that day, Yahweh entered into covenant with Abram" (v. 18). There are different kinds of covenants mentioned in Scripture.[23] Some are *parity covenants*—that is, agreements between equals. These are contracts in which human beings voluntarily come together to agree to make certain promises to each other, and each party expresses their commitment to keep those promises for as long as they agree the contract shall be in force. If either party proves to be disloyal to their contractual obligations, the contract is considered violated and nullified. Parity agreements can be made between individuals (1 Samuel 18:3–4; 23:18; Psalm 55:20), households (Genesis 31:43–54), and even nations (Hosea 12:1; Obadiah 7). Marriage is an example of a parity covenant (Proverbs 2:17; Malachi 2:14).

A second kind of covenant appearing in Scripture is a *suzerainty covenant*. This is a covenant between unequals. The superior party imposes the agreement (Jeremiah 34:8–10; Ezekiel 17:12–14), grants it (1 Samuel 11:1–2), or guarantees it (Joshua 9:6–15).

The third kind of covenant is called a *promissory covenant* or a *suzerainty testament*. This is also a covenant between unequals. It can be a promise made by the lesser party to the greater party, for instance, to support a new king (2 Kings 11:4–11) or to obey God's written Word (23:1–3). More often in Scripture, God is the one who makes the covenant with human beings and assures them with various promises that he will keep it. It's this kind of covenant that's in view in Genesis 15:18. Yahweh promises Abram that his descendants will occupy the designated land. This is a covenant of grace; Abram has done nothing to earn the gift it offers, nor can he. God makes the covenant, and he alone guarantees it. "It is a promissory oath made by God alone."[24]

EXPERIENCE GOD'S HEART

God keeps his promises. He may not keep them on our time-table or even according to the way we would like, but he never fails to keep his word. If he has said he will do something, we can count on him to do it.

- Genesis is just one of the sixty-six books of Scripture that record God's faithfulness to his word. Lean into him and his promises. Trust him to fulfill what he has said he would do. Do this before him right now. Prayerfully commit yourself to him and his commit-ment to you. Consider, too, what the apostle Paul says about what we, who are in Christ, can expect God to do for us, especially given what he has already done for us (Romans 8). Revel and relax in God's love. He is for you—forever!

Sarai and Hagar

Genesis 16 concerns not God's land promise to Abram but his promise of heirs. And this time, Abram is not the impatient one; his wife Sarai is.

The Scheme

- *According to the account, what is the situation, the problem it raises, and Sarai's solution (16:1–2)?*

- *Now God had promised several times that Abram would have children. And yet, what does Abram do when Sarai comes to him with her plan (v. 2)? How much older was Abram at this time and, by implication, Sarai (v. 3; cf. v. 16)?*

- *What do you learn about Hagar and her relationship to Sarai in verses 1–3?*

- *How does Abram respond to Sarai's scheme (vv. 2, 4)?*

# THE BACKSTORY

According to Gordon Wenham:

> It was a serious matter for a man to be childless in the ancient world, for it left him without an heir. But it was even more calamitous for a woman: to have a great brood of children was the mark of success as a wife; to have none was ignominious failure. So throughout the ancient East polygamy was resorted to as a means of obviating childlessness. But wealthier wives preferred the practice of surrogate motherhood, whereby they allowed their husbands to "go in to"...their maids, a euphemism for sexual intercourse (cf. [Genesis] 6:4; 30:3; 38:8, 9; 39:14). The mistress could then feel that her maid's child was her own and exert some control over it in a way that she could not if her husband simply took a second wife.[25]

- Let's compare Genesis 3 with chapter 16.

What did Eve offer to her husband (3:6)?

What did Sarai offer to her husband (16:2)?

What did Eve think her offering would accomplish (3:6)?

What did Sarai think her offering would accomplish (16:2)?

What was Adam's response to Eve (3:6)?

What was Abram's response to Sarai (16:2, 4)?

What did Eve's and Adam's choices violate (2:16–17)?

What did Sarai's and Abram's choices violate (2:24; 12:2; 13:15–16; 15:4–5)?

Remember Abram's choice not to rely on God for protection when he went into Egypt but to hatch a deception instead (12:11–13)? Sarai hatched her own scheme as well, showing that she didn't trust God to deliver either. But this time it wasn't physical protection at issue, though it still had to do with failing to have faith in God's promise to give them countless descendants. If one or both of them were dead, then they couldn't have children. Likewise, if Sarai remained childless, then she and Abram would not have children either. So Sarai took it upon herself to find a way to fulfill God's promise of descendants while she and her husband still lived.

The Fallout

Just as Abram's plan in Egypt reaped initial success (12:14–16), so did Sarai's plan to use Hagar. Hagar became pregnant (16:4). But the joy didn't last.

- *What did Hagar do when she realized she was pregnant (16:4)?*

- *What did Sarai do as a result (v. 5)?*

- *What did Abram do to try to soften the blow for Sarai, and how did she follow Abram's advice (v. 6)?*

- *What do you think of Abram's response to his wife? Consider: Abram now had two wives, Sarai and Hagar. He also had a child by his second wife, both of whom should have been worthy of his protection. Instead, he attempts to placate Sarai. What is your assessment of Abram's actions?*

- *How did Sarai now treat Hagar, and what did that lead Hagar to do (v. 6)?*

𝕳 WORD WEALTH

The Hebrew term translated "cruelly mistreated" is "used to describe the suffering endured by the Israelites in Egypt in [Gen.] 15:13; Exod 1:12. So intolerable was her [Hagar's] suffering that she ran away…, another term used of the Israelites leaving Egypt (Exod 14:5) but very frequently used of people escaping from attempts to kill them ([Gen.] 27:43; 35:1; Exod 2:15; 1 Sam 19:12, 18)."[26]

Deliverance

The situation looks bleak. Just as the situation in Egypt soured for Abram and Sarai, so did Sarai's plan to have a child through Hagar. Sarai lost her maidservant, Hagar lost her home, and Abram lost his second wife and newborn child.

Hagar fled south, toward her home nation of Egypt. While "by a spring in the wilderness" (Genesis 16:7), the angel of Yahweh comes to her. He clearly knows her and asks her from where she has come and what she is doing in this place.

- *Does Hagar answer the angel's question honestly (Genesis 16:8)?*

- *What is the angel's response, and what promise did he make her (vv. 9–10)?*

- *How does the angel's promise to Hagar compare to what Yahweh had told Abram about his descendants (13:16)?*

- *What does the angel say about Hagar's son (16:11–12)?*

- *After the angel left her, to whom did Hagar realize that she had been speaking (vv. 13–14)? Support your answer from the text.*

- *Did Hagar obey what Yahweh had told her to do (v. 15)?*

- *Notice that Sarai is not mentioned at all in the last two verses of Genesis 16. Instead, the focus is on Hagar, Abram, and their son Ishmael. Why do you think Sarai goes unnamed here?*

DIGGING DEEPER

The "angel of Yahweh (Lord)" is mentioned fifty-eight times in the Old Testament, and the "angel of God" occurs eleven times.[27] We must use the context of these phrases to discover whether the angel mentioned is actually an appearance of the Lord God. Hagar certainly believed she had encountered God, and no one but God could keep the promise that he made to her about her descendants. In Judges, Gideon encounters the angel of Yahweh, whom the writer identifies as Yahweh and Gideon later realizes was Yahweh (Judges 6:11–24). This divine presence in angelic form also appeared to a man named Manoah and his wife, and they, too, later realized that they had encountered God (13:2–24).

In almost every case that this angel appears, he's first mistaken to be a man and only later grasped to be God himself.

Who was he? The church fathers believed he was the pre-incarnate Son of God, and many Bible scholars today accept that interpretation as well. In other words, when the angel of Yahweh appears in Genesis 16 and elsewhere, he is none other than God the Son, Christ himself. Such appearances are called "Christophanies," and these would have likely been some of the many passages Jesus would have gone to when he showed two disciples from the writings of "Moses and all the prophets...the revelation of himself throughout the Scriptures" (Luke 24:27).

After presenting some of the evidence for identifying the angel of Yahweh as Christ, theologian Norman L. Geisler observes: "once the Son (Christ) came in permanent incarnate form (John 1:1, 14; 1 John 4:2), never again does *the* Angel of the Lord appear, though *an* angel appears from time to time (cf. Acts 12:7ff.). *No angel that commands or accepts worship or claims to be God ever appears again.*"[28]

What's Ahead?

Genesis 16 ends with God's promise of heirs to Abram left unfulfilled. Ishmael does not fulfill the promise, although God still blesses Hagar and her descendants. When will the initial heir for Abram come? How much longer must he wait? Abram and Sarai are not getting any younger, and both have expressed impatience at different times. The next section of Genesis we explore will finally answer these questions. Yahweh will keep his word—but in his way and according to his timetable.

Talking It Out

1. The eternal, all-knowing God takes the long view as he carries out his plans. This can lead us to become impatient and frustrated as we wait on him and even find ways, as Abram and Sarai did, to hurry God's plans along. What are some steps we can take that will help us wait upon him rather than take matters into our own hands?

2. Provide a character portrait of Abram and then Sarai based upon what you have learned about each person so far. What do their words and actions reveal about them?

3. Up to this point in Genesis and throughout the rest of the book, nations, tribes, families, couples, and individuals fulfill various aspects of God's plans. Sometimes they obey his will, while other times they don't. And yet God continues to work through them, around them, in spite of them, and even against them to carry out his will—and all without failing to love them, continuing to do what's good for them. What does this tell you about God's sovereignty and faithfulness? Is he showing that he can be trusted and relied upon?

LESSON 3

Revelation, Sign, and Judgment

(17:1–19:38)

A promise kept; faith honored.
Faith tested and found true.
More divine revelation comes.
More blessing is poured out.
More sin brings divine judgment.
Family is enlarged while loss is endured.

The drama of the Book of Beginnings continues with Abram's and Sarai's story. Aspects of Yahweh's promises to them and their descendants see some more fulfillment even while a broken world shows more signs of its ongoing decline into decadence. God keeps showing that he will not abandon his image bearers even when his justice demands satisfaction.

An Everlasting Covenant and Its Sign

"When Abram was ninety-nine years old, Yahweh appeared to him again" (Genesis 17:1). Thirteen years had passed since the close of the events recorded in chapter 16. Sarai was now eighty-nine and Ishmael thirteen. We don't know Hagar's age. During this divine encounter, Yahweh confirms his promissory covenant—a covenant between unequals—with Abram.

- *How does Yahweh identify himself to Abram (17:1)?*

- *What does Yahweh say he's about to do (v. 2)?*

- *How does Abram initially respond to Yahweh's presence (v. 3)?*

- *What are the central details of Yahweh's covenant with Abram, including what Abram and Sarai are supposed to do to uphold their part of the agreement (vv. 4–16)?*

- *What is the significance of the name changes for Abram and Sarai (vv. 5, 15; see TPT study notes on these verses too)?*

- *What is Abraham's response to hearing Yahweh's promise that the prophet and Sarah would have children (vv. 17–18)?*

- *What is God's answer to Abraham (vv. 19–21)?*

- *Read study note 'c' for verse 19 and then write out what the name "Isaac" means. Why do you think the promised son was to receive this name?*

- *Where does God go after his exchange with Abraham (v. 22)?*

- *What action does Abraham take after God leaves him (vv. 23–27)?*

Imagine what it would have been like to have been a member of Abraham's household, to have served him for many years, and then to have him announce to you and to everyone else who served him that your quite aged master was now to be called Abraham, "the father of a multitude," and Sarai was now to be called Sarah, which served to emphasize her ongoing role as princess or queen in the family. At this point, all the children they had were one: Ishmael. And Abraham and Sarah were advanced in age, well beyond the physical ability to have children of their own. Furthermore, you hear Abraham announce that all the males, including himself, would have to be circumcised—a painful and intimate procedure, to be sure.

- *What do you imagine you would have thought about all of this?*

- *Do you think you would have gone along with these changes? Why or why not?*

 EXPERIENCE GOD'S HEART

- *Has God ever asked you to trust him in some way that put you on the line with others you knew? Record your story.*

- *How did his request work out for you and for those who knew you?*

- *Would you trust God again with a revelation he gave specifically to you? Why or why not?*

Heavenly Guests and Deserved Destruction

Genesis 18 opens with yet another appearance of Yahweh to Abraham "while he lived by the oak grove of Mamre" (v. 1). This time Yahweh, who looked like a man, had two other human-male-appearing figures with him (v. 2).

- *What did Abraham do for his three male guests (18:2–8)?*

The four men sharing a meal together conveys "intimate fellowship. To eat together was important for fellowship, peace offerings, and treaties. When the Lord was ready to specify the fulfillment of the covenantal promise, He came in person and ate in Abraham's tent. Nothing could more significantly communicate their close relationship."[29] And yet, while this event displayed fellowship, Abraham stood rather than sitting with his three guests while they ate. This suggests that Abraham knew who his guests were, so he honored them, not just with food but also with his posture before them.

- At the end of the meal, what did the guests ask Abraham (v. 9)?

- Since Sarah had not appeared to the guests up to this point in the story and no one had mentioned her, how did they know her name?

- One of the guests then announced something that would soon occur. What did he say? Where was Sarah, and how did she react to the guest's announcement (vv. 10–12)?

- What exchange followed between Yahweh, Abraham, and Sarah (vv. 13–15)?

• *How do you suppose Yahweh knew what Sarah thought?*

With the meal over and Yahweh's emphatic promise that Abraham and Sarah would soon have their promised son, Isaac, Abraham accompanied Yahweh and the other two guests as they walked toward Lot's chosen city of Sodom (v. 16).

• *Summarize what Yahweh tells Abraham (vv. 17–21).*

• *Do you think that God, who knows a person's thoughts and makes promises about the future that he always keeps, already knows what he will find in Sodom? If so, why would God speak to Abraham this way? Jot down your thoughts.*

- *Abraham then chooses to bargain with Yahweh as the other two men continue to Sodom (vv. 22–32). What does Abraham want Yahweh to do and why? What is it about Yahweh that gives Abraham confidence that he can even get a hearing for his case, much less "win over" Yahweh?*

- *What is the conclusion of the bargaining session? What is it that Yahweh tells Abraham that he will finally do (v. 32)?*

Genesis 19:1 finally specifies that the other two men with Yahweh were angels.

- *Whom did they meet when they arrived at Sodom, and what did this citizen of the city do for the human-looking angels (19:2–3)?*

- How did the other men of the city reward Lot's hospitality toward the strangers (vv. 4–5)?

- What was Lot's response to the crowd's demand, and how did they answer Lot's counteroffer (vv. 6–9)?

- What does Lot's plea to the crowd reveal about his judgment on their demands?

- What was Lot attempting to prevent and safeguard by making his shocking offer of appeasement to the crowd? Do you agree or disagree with Lot's decision? Support your answer.

- *What was the angels' response to Lot's failed attempt to appease his fellow Sodomites (vv. 10–13)?*

- *How many people left with Lot before God's judgment came upon Sodom (vv. 14–16)? Who were they?*

- *What did the angels tell Lot and his family to do once they were out of the city, and what compromise did Lot ask them to make (vv. 17–22)?*

- *What happened after "Lot arrived at the small village of Zoar" (v. 23; cf. vv. 24–29)?*

💙 SHARE GOD'S HEART

Are you living or working in a place marked far more by vice than by virtue? It may not be as wicked as were Sodom and Gomorrah, but if it has chosen to go its own way rather than God's, it is in moral and spiritual decline as were those ancient cities. Ask God how you can be his man or woman where you are so you can shine his light in darkness. Then remain open to his lead. He may still set that place aside for judgment, but you may lead some people out into a future that's full of his light rather than the bleakness of human sin.

Deceptions and Conceptions

The story of Lot, Abraham's nephew, comes to a close in the final verses of Genesis 19. His name never comes up again in Scripture until 2 Peter 2:6–9. Genesis 19 does not leave us with a good impression of Lot and his family.

- *Where does the once prosperous and wealthy Lot end up with his daughters (Genesis 19:30; cf. 13:5–11)?*

- *What plan do Lot's daughters hatch and for what reason (vv. 31–32)?*

- *Did their plan work, and what nations came out of their actions (vv. 33–38)?*

Lot's choice to walk by sight rather than by faith when he left Abram for more lush land in Genesis 13 eventually led him to establish his home in the decadent city of Sodom. Then, writes Bible commentator Bruce Waltke:

> He [Lot] tries to be a host and father but fails to offer his guests real safety or his family decisive leadership. The story of Lot's offer of his daughters seems to reveal Lot as sincerely desiring to do right, but failing miserably. So corrupted by the city he had embraced, he offers an equally immoral act to stop an atrocity.
>
> The desperate scheme by Lot's daughters to preserve seed from their drunken father brings to a conclusion the tragic account of Lot, which began with his separation from Abraham. In spite of Lot's affiliation with Sodom and the unbelief of his family, the Lord mercifully protects his lineage and land (see Deut. 2:16–19) because of Lot's condemnation of the wickedness of the men of Sodom (2 Peter 2:7–8), his hospitality to strangers, and his relationship to Abraham.[30]

 THE BACKSTORY

The Moabites and Ammonites who descended from Lot's unnamed daughters later became enemies of Israel (Numbers 23–25; 2 Kings 3). And God later rejected them because of their poor treatment of Israel (Deuteronomy 23:3–6).[31] Nevertheless, from the Moabites would come Ruth and, from her line, Israel's King David and eventually God's incarnate Son, Jesus Christ (Ruth 4:13–22; Matthew 1:5–6, 16).

Talking It Out

1. Almost two thousand years after the life of Abraham, the apostle Paul wrote, "If you belong to Christ, then you are now Abraham's 'child' and a true heir of all his blessings because of the promise God made to Abraham!" (Galatians 3:29). We Christians are sons and daughters of God's promise to Abraham. We are members of the nations God has blessed, and we have become Abraham's heirs through faith in the promised seed who came down to us from him. Talk about God keeping his promises! When have you relied on God's promises? How did God honor your faith? How has that worked in your ongoing relationship with God? For example, has it strengthened your faith? Has it led you to turn to God more often? Has it deepened your understanding of God and how he works?

2. The sin and destruction of Sodom and Gomorrah in Genesis 19 receive comment in other biblical passages. Read through Deuteronomy 32:28–33; Isaiah 3:8–9; Matthew 10:11–15; Luke 17:28–30; 2 Peter 2:6–10; and Jude 7. What do you learn about the sins of these cities and how they continued to be repeated and even surpassed? What is God's judgment on such evil?

3. Our choices have consequences, sometimes for our good and sometimes not for our good. When Lot chose to part company with Abraham and settle himself and his family near Sodom (Genesis 13:12–13), he may not have realized at the time that the place he chose had become "extremely wicked" (v. 13). But once there for a while, he surely recognized the dreadful condition of the people. Still, he chose to stay rather than to leave. Through that decision, he eventually lost his home and some of his family, including his wife. Talk about one or more decisions you have made that had negative consequences. What have you learned from those decisions that have helped you make better ones?

LESSON 4

Isaac, the Promised Son

(20:1–23:20)

Before the promised child arrives to Abraham and Sarah, the couple leaves Mamre and travels to southern Canaan. There they settle for a while in Gerar, which was a "Philistine city-kingdom south of Gaza" (Genesis 20:1).[32] While there, Abraham pulls the same deception with the king of Gerar that he had done with Pharaoh when he was in Egypt.

- *What did Abraham say about Sarah, and what did that lead Gerar's king, Abimelech, to do (20:2)?*

- *What did God do to protect Sarah, and how did Abimelech respond to God (vv. 3–7)?*

- *Summarize what Abimelech did the next morning and what Abraham said to justify his deception (vv. 8–13).*

- *How did Abimelech choose to make the situation right, how did Abraham respond, and how did God answer (vv. 14–18)?*

Finally, the promised son arrived.

- *Summarize the story of Isaac's arrival and how his parents responded to it (21:1–7).*

- *How old were Abraham and Sarah when Isaac was born?*

Still in Abraham's household was the son he had by Hagar. As Hagar had mocked Sarah many years before (16:4), now Hagar's son made fun of Isaac (21:9).

- *How did Sarah respond to Ishmael's treatment of Isaac (21:10)?*

- *What was Abraham's response, and what direction did God give him (vv. 11–13)?*

- *Did Abraham follow God's guidance (v. 14)?*

- *How did all of this work out for Hagar and Ishmael (vv. 14–21)?*

- *While God stuck with his plan A for Abraham and Sarah and their chosen seed, he still blessed their plan B in some ways. What does this reveal about God's love for his image bearers? And what does it tell you about God's commitment to his plan rather than ours?*

A Covenant among Equals

The rest of Genesis 21 tells us about a covenant that King Abimelech and Abraham freely entered into to protect each other's interests. Although Abimelech was royalty, so in that way superior to Abraham, the king recognized that Abraham was a special recipient of divine blessing. He approached Abraham as a friend, as an equal, so their agreement with one another was a parity covenant.

- *When Abimelech approached Abraham, what did he want from the prophet (vv. 22–23)?*

- *Summarize Abraham's response to the king (vv. 24–31).*

- *After the covenant was complete and the king had left, Abraham turned to God. What were the prophet's specific actions? And what was the sign that the covenant with Abimelech was effective (vv. 33–34)?*

A Test of Faith

Faith never goes untested. Testing proves faith, refines it, develops it, and strengthens it. Abraham had already demonstrated his faith in God on several occasions, and he had stopped to worship him as well. In Genesis 22, Abraham receives his greatest test—one that concerns his promised son, Isaac, and one that will demonstrate Abraham's commitment to God and his promises.

The passage opens by telling us that the story about to be told occurred "some time later" after Abraham's covenant with Abimelech and after sending his other son, Ishmael, away (22:1). Waltke speculates that at least a decade had passed since Isaac had been weaned because he was now strong enough to carry the wood for the sacrifice (20:8; 22:6).[33]

- *The writer says that God came to Abraham to test him (22:1). What was the test? What did God want Abraham to do (v. 2)?*

- *What would such a test prove about Abraham?*

Moriah was about fifty miles north of Beersheba, the place where Abraham began his journey to the region (v. 19). Moriah centuries later became the location of Jerusalem's temple mount (2 Chronicles 3:1), where countless sacrifices were made in obedience to the Mosaic law. The God who created human beings, breathed life into them, and stamped his image upon them calls on Abraham to snuff out one of those lives. And the life God designates is Isaac, the very son that Abraham and Sarah had waited to receive for twenty-five years. From Sarah's dead womb, the longed-for son was conceived and born. God had promised him, and God had fulfilled his promise. Now he wanted Abraham to sacrifice his son. Would the aged Abraham perform the deed? Would he kill his only son from Sarah, the son he so dearly loved, the divinely promised child?

- *After God revealed his will to Abraham, what action did this elderly father take (Genesis 22:3–10)?*

- *What do Abraham's words in verses 5 and 8 convey to you about his expectations?*

- *As Abraham was about to kill his son, what happened (vv. 11–13)?*

- *What name did Abraham give to that mountain of sacrifice (v. 14)?*

- *The angel of Yahweh—who identified himself as Yahweh—then pronounced a blessing upon Abraham (vv. 16–18). What was Yahweh's blessing?*

🫀 EXPERIENCE GOD'S HEART

Since the angel of Yahweh was the preincarnate Son appearing in angelic form, understand that he was God's only Son, the beloved of the heavenly Father, who told Abraham to sacrifice his only son, Isaac. One day the Son became the sacrifice for the sins of the world, and in his humanity, he was a physical and spiritual descendant of Abraham. Through Abraham's seed, then, the Son has brought the greatest blessing of all upon the whole world. All we have to do is receive the blessing of his sacrifice by faith (John 3:13–18; Romans 10:8–13).

- *Have you trusted in God's Son? Have you accepted the fact that he has paid your debt to God, and have you put your faith in him for this (Galatians 3:6–14; Colossians 2:13–14)? If you haven't, please do that now. Just call on Yahweh to forgive you of your sins because of what Jesus has done for you on the cross. Ask him to save you, and he will. If you have already put your faith in Jesus Christ, then take time now to offer up your praise and thanksgiving for all he has already done for you.*

🫶 SHARE GOD'S HEART

Our "Savior-God...longs for everyone to embrace his life and return to the full knowledge of the truth," which includes the facts that "God is one, and there is one Mediator between God and the sons of men—the true man, Jesus, the Anointed One" who "gave himself as ransom-payment for everyone" (1 Timothy 2:3–6).

- *With whom can you share these truths this week or next? Write down their names below and then commit to praying for them, asking our Savior-God to prepare their hearts for your time with them. Be sure to pray that he works within you also, so you will be sensitive to what you say to them and how. Jesus varied his dealings with men and women depending on who they were and what they needed. His disciples learned from him and did the same.[34] The truth doesn't vary, but how we communicate it can and should.*

Family Expansion and Loss

The rest of Genesis 22 is good news for Abraham and Sarah. They receive news that their extended family has grown by quite a bit. Eight more nephews were added through Milcah and Abraham's brother, Nahor (Genesis 22:20). And four more came through Nahor and his other wife, Reumah.

- *List the names of the sons who came from Milcah and, if mentioned, their relationship to other family members (vv. 21–22).*

- *Select any two of the sons to research. See The Passion Translation study notes for help. Also consult a Bible study resource on such sites as biblegateway.com or biblehub.com. Record below what you find.*

- *Now refer to TPT study note 'j' on Rebekah. Who was she? You may also want to refer to another Bible resource on one of the websites mentioned previously.*

- *Here list the names of Reumah's four sons (v. 24). Pick one to research further.*

THE BACKSTORY

According to Waltke:

> This genealogy completes the details of the
> descendants of Nahor and Milcah (11:29)
> and sets the stage for the introduction
> of Rebekah into the family line of the
> patriarchs (24:1–67; cf. 25:20)...
>
> The twelve nonelect sons of Nahor, who
> probably become tribes, parallel the twelve
> elect sons/tribes of Abraham through his
> grandson Jacob. In each case, there are
> eight by the principal wife/wives and four
> from the secondary wife/wives (22:20, 24;
> 29:31–30:24; 35:16–18). The number twelve
> also matches the twelve sons/tribes of
> Ishmael (see 17:20; 25:12–16).[35]

Other features of the tight narrative structure of the patriarchal stories are expressed by commentator Gordon Wenham:

> It may be noted that the stories of
> Abraham, Isaac, and Jacob all conclude
> with a similar sequence: promise
> (22:15–18; 35:9–14; 48:4), journey (22:19;
> 35:16; 48:7), birth of children (22:20–24;
> 35:17–18; 48:5–6), and death and burial
> of patriarch's wife (chap. 23; 35:18–20;
> 48:7)...These parallels show that the author
> of this material worked according to a
> coherent scheme.[36]

While Genesis 22 ends with new life in Abraham's extended family, chapter 23 focuses on the death of his long-time partner in life, Sarah. Genesis reiterates over and over the many ways death has entered into God's creation through the rebellion of the first human pair. Here in chapter 23, Moses reminds his readers that even the most faithful followers of Yahweh are not immune to sin's consequences.

- How old was Sarah when she died (23:1)?

- How did Abraham respond to losing his wife (v. 2)?

- The rest of the chapter tells how Abraham found and purchased a burial site for Sarah and other family members (vv. 3–20). Read through the account and answer the questions that follow:

    In what land and near which city was Sarah buried (v. 19)?

    Who had owned the land that became Sarah's burial site (v. 20)?

    Canaan was the promised land, and although God said it would go to Abraham and his descendants, how did Abraham see his relationship to Canaan and its people (v. 4)?

With Abraham's purchase of land for Sarah's burial site, the first patriarch of Israel finally had a legal claim in Canaan, the land of divine promise. He also had a resting place for the first mother of all the descendants yet to come, a woman who also was his companion through most of his life. Of this burial site, Wenham remarks:

> It was in a place associated with some of her [Sarah's] happiest memories. It was at Mamre that the Lord had promised her that she would give birth to a child within the year (18:1–15). Indeed, most of the great promises of land, descendants, and covenant blessing seem to be associated with their years in Mamre, according to 13:14–18:15. And in a sense the purchase of the plot of land at Macpelah was a first step toward Abraham and his descendants' acquisition of the whole land of Canaan. For this reason, Genesis draws attention twice to the rather obvious point that Hebron is in the land of Canaan (23:2, 19) and repeatedly insists that the negotiations and payment for the land were conducted publicly before the elders of the city (vv. 10, 13, 16, 18). There was no doubt that this part of Canaan justly belonged to Abraham and his heirs.[37]

Talking It Out

1. The near sacrifice of Isaac displays Abraham's great faith commitment to God. On a scale of one to ten, with one the lowest and ten the highest, where would you rank your level of faith in God and why? What would it take for your faith in him to increase?

2. When we hear the story of Abraham's call to sacrifice Isaac, we don't often think of what must have gone through Isaac's mind as he journeyed with his father to Moriah, carried the wood to the place of sacrifice, and experienced his father preparing him for the altar. Review this account in Genesis 22 and focus on Isaac. What details does the text present that provide some insight into Isaac's state of mind and heart? If you had been young Isaac, what do you suppose you would have felt and thought during this episode in your life? What does Isaac's compliance convey to you about his trust in his father and in God?

3. The loss of a loved one is always difficult to bear. In the section of Genesis that we covered in this lesson and the previous one, Lot lost his wife, and Abraham lost his. Lot's came to an end through divine judgment, while Abraham's died due to advanced age. No matter how or why a loved one leaves us, we experience grief. What has been your experience with the death of someone close? How did you handle it? What are some of the ways you may still feel the absence of that person from your life? How has your relationship to God helped? Did any others reach out to you in comforting, beneficial ways? What did you learn about enduring and overcoming grief that you would use to help others?

LESSON 5

Securing Isaac's Future

24:1–25:18

When Sarah died, she was 127 years old. Since Abraham was a decade older than she, he was 137 at the time. Only God knew how much longer Abraham would live. And the patriarch needed to ensure that his son Isaac would have a wife who would also give him children. God had promised Abraham descendants, but the prophet only had one through whom God said he would continue his blessing.

When Sarah delivered Isaac, she was ninety years old (Genesis 17:17). When she passed away at 127, Isaac was a man of thirty-seven years. He wasn't growing younger, and Abraham wasn't either. It was time for Isaac to have a wife and make a home for his own family.

A Wife for Isaac

Abraham's Charge

After acknowledging how wonderfully and generously Yahweh had blessed Abraham (24:1), Moses tells the story of the events Abraham began that successfully led to a wife for Isaac.

- Read the account of Abraham's interaction with his "head servant" concerning his charge to the servant to find a proper bride for Isaac (24:2–9). Answer the following questions:

  What was the servant supposed to accomplish for Abraham?

  Where was the servant told to go to accomplish his mission, and what area was he told to avoid?

  Whom did Abraham believe would give the servant success and on what basis?

  To solidify the servant's commitment to the assigned task, what did Abraham ask him to do? (See TPT's study note 'd' for 24:2 for additional information.) Did the servant comply with Abraham's insistence (v. 9)?

The Servant's Success

- *With the oath taken between Abraham and his servant, the servant leaves on his journey. What does he take with him (v. 10)?*

- *Where does he go, and how far did he travel (v. 10; see also the study notes on this verse)?*

- *Now in the village of Abraham's brother, what does the servant do to try to secure a successful mission (vv. 11–14)?*

- *Who comes to the well, what is she like, and does she actually fulfill the requirements of the servant's proposed sign (vv. 15–20)?*

- *How does the servant respond to what happens at the well (vv. 21–27)?*

- *How does the servant end up at Rebekah's house (vv. 28–31)?*

- *Once the servant arrives at the house, how is he treated (vv. 32–33)?*

- *The servant then tells Laban, Rebekah, and the rest of their family why he has come and how he came to meet Rebekah (vv. 34–50). As you read this part of the story, record anything you find that provides more information or insight than the writer gave before.*

- *How did Rebekah and her family respond to the servant's story (vv. 51–61)?*

- *To whom did the servant give credit for his success, and how did he show this (vv. 52, 56)?*

EXPERIENCE GOD'S HEART

At some time or another, we will find ourselves under the authority of another person who will require or request something of us that will take a lot of effort to fulfill and perhaps some personal sacrifices. If we choose to honor what's been asked of us, we would be wise to do so with God's help, as Abraham's head servant clearly did when he prayed, "Yahweh, God of my master Abraham, let my journey here be a success and show your gracious love to my master Abraham" (24:12). Many centuries later, the apostle Paul confirmed this servant's approach to fulfilling Abraham's request: "Serve your employers wholeheartedly and with love, as though you were serving Christ and not men" (Ephesians 6:7).

- *Have you been approached to perform a task that may require much from you? If so, what is it?*

- *Are you willing to fulfill what's been asked as though "you were serving Christ and not men"? Why or why not?*

- *Christ was asked by his heavenly Father to leave behind his glory, become one of us, live among us, teach us and serve us, and then die for us. It was not an easy mission to accomplish, and yet Christ did it willingly and without complaint (Philippians 2:5–9; Hebrews 2:14–18; 4:15). Are you willing to follow his example? If you are, "Be assured that anything you do that is beautiful and excellent will be repaid by our Lord" (Ephesians 6:8).*

Isaac Marries

Abraham's servant and his entourage guided Rebekah and her attendants along the long journey from Nahor's village in Mesopotamia to "the southern desert of Canaan" (Genesis 24:61–62)—a trek that would have taken a month or more.[38]

- *When Abraham's servant and Rebekah were close, where was Isaac, and what was he doing (24:63; cf. study note 'f')?*

• *Read verses 64–67 and summarize what you learn,*
  especially about the initial meeting between Isaac and
  Rebekah and to what that led.

The Unchosen Line

With the story of Isaac's marriage told, Moses turns to giving an account of another wife of Abraham and the sons produced from that marriage.

• As you read through 25:1–4, write down the names of the sons that came from the union of Abraham and Keturah. Use the headings below to order your list:

Sons of Abraham and Keturah:

Sons of Jokshan:

Sons of Dedan:

Sons of Midian:

- *Choose at least one of the descendants listed to research further in another Bible study resource (e.g., a Bible dictionary, Bible encyclopedia, or Bible online resource). Jot down what you learn below.*

- *Although Abraham ended up having many more children after Isaac and Ishmael, he protected Isaac and the divine promises about his son by doing what (vv. 6–7)?*

 SHARE GOD'S HEART

Sometimes "chosenness" in Scripture refers to those who are spiritually saved, such as when the apostle Paul says of God the Father that "in love he chose us before he laid the foundation of the universe...For it was always in his perfect plan to adopt us as his delightful children, through our union with Jesus" (Ephesians 1:4–5).

At other times, however, such as in Genesis, the chosen line of Eve's seed that came through Seth, Shem, Abraham, and Isaac concerns the *physical* lineage of the one who would become the incarnate Messiah. Chosenness in this sense has no direct bearing on the salvific status of anyone in the line of descendants.

Spiritual salvation has always come the same way—by faith in him who saves. Paul makes this very point in his treatise on the gospel, Romans. He harks back to Abraham and asks what made this "founder of Judaism…right with God" (Romans 4:1–2). His answer was to refer back to Genesis 15:6: "Listen to what the Scriptures say: Because Abraham believed God's words, his faith transferred God's righteousness into his account" (Romans 4:3). Faith is the means of salvation; faith is what confers on us a right standing before God. Salvation has nothing to do with our family of origin, our social standing, our "good" deeds, or anything else we can offer or do. Salvation comes by faith alone.

Now, does saving faith produce good works? Absolutely! As James says, saving faith is never alone but always exhibits its reality through our obedience to God (James 2:14–25). In other words, true faith is a working faith; it bears the fruit of faith. But it is still faith and only faith by which we are saved!

Spiritual salvation comes through the triune God—Father, Son, and Holy Spirit. God the Father is the source of salvation (Romans 8:28–30, 32; Ephesians 1:4–5, 11; 1 Peter 1:2). God the Son accomplishes the work of salvation (Romans 3:21–26). And God the Spirit secures that salvation within us (Romans 8:9–16; Ephesians 1:13–14). But salvation remains ineffective or unapplied until we trust in him who saves, the Lord Jesus Christ (Acts 4:10–12; John 3:16–18; 14:6; Romans 4:22–5:2).

So if anyone asks you, "Are you chosen of God?," you can answer, "Yes, I am, by my faith in Jesus Christ. And you can be chosen, too, if you put your faith in Jesus."

 # THE BACKSTORY

The chronology of Abraham's marriage to Keturah is uncertain. He may have married her after Sarah's death, in which case their children would have been born during the last forty years of Abraham's life, roughly between his age of 137 and 175. If this is so, then it shows "the extreme blessedness of Abraham's old age.

He who had such difficulty fathering one son earlier in his life now enjoys new procreativity in his latter years." [39]

It's also possible that Abraham was married to Keturah while Sarah was still alive. First Chronicles 1:32 refers to Keturah as Abraham's concubine, and Genesis 25:6 seems to designate Keturah as a concubine. If this is the case, then Abraham engaged in the practice of polygamy. Polygamy was a common practice in the ancient world, and it was apparently first introduced by the depraved Lamech (Genesis 4:19). God's design for marriage was for one man and one woman to marry and remain exclusive to each other (2:18–25). But even otherwise godly men sometimes did not heed this ideal. Abraham showed himself willing to engage in polygamy when he followed Sarah's desire to have a child by Hagar.

Regardless of when Abraham married Keturah and had children with her, she and their offspring most likely ended up settling in the "vast territory east of Israel extending from the Middle Euphrates to Arabia."[40] While this places them outside of the promised land, their association with Abraham further shows how this patriarch became the father of many nations (17:4–6).

Abraham's Death

Genesis 25:7–11 records the death of Israel's first patriarch, Abraham.

• *How old was Abraham when he died, and who buried him?*

- *Where was Abraham buried?*

- *How did Isaac fare after his father died, and where did he settle?*

- *What was the significance of the place where Isaac chose to live (see 16:7–14; 24:62–67; and note 'g' in TPT for 25:11)?*

Ishmael's Line and Death

Book 7 in Genesis is short. It covers the descendants (*toledot*) of Ishmael and his death (25:12–18). This is the line that started with Abraham and Hagar (v. 12), and it is not part of the chosen line, but because it is linked with Abraham, the writer covers it before returning to the chosen heritage that came from Abraham, Sarah, and Isaac.

- *How many sons did Ishmael have, and who were they (25:13–15)?*

- *Each son became the source of a tribe (v. 16; cf. 17:20). What territory did these tribes settle in (25:17–18)?*

- *How does the writer characterize Ishmael's life, and what was his age when he died (25:17–18; cf. 16:12)?*

# THE BACKSTORY

That Ishmael's descendants formed twelve tribes is significant in Genesis and in the larger scope of biblical history. As Waltke explains:

> Surely the mention of the twelve tribes of Arameans [Gen. 22:20–23], of Ishmaelites [25:12–16], of Edomites [36:9–14], and of Israelites [35:23–26] is not fortuitous. Christ even chooses twelve apostles, symbolic of the twelve tribes of Israel (Matt. 19:28; Luke 22:30; Rev. 21:12–14). The number twelve seems to represent God's ordering of creation and history, demonstrated by the fact that twelve is a basic unit for measuring time and organizing history (e.g., 24 hours [12 x 2] and 144 as the ideal number of the eschatological kingdom [12 x 12]). This suggests that all these tribes, one from Abraham's brother Nahor and three from his own loins, participate in God's common grace and elective purposes. The merciful God increases all of them and uniquely blesses Ishmael with longevity and a great nation (Gen. 17:20). Moreover, the Sovereign will later use these tribal confederacies to discipline his elect people. They also will be disciplined for their contentious spirit and fierce pride (cf. Isa. 21:13–17; Jer. 49:28–33). Ultimately, the gracious Sovereign will bring all under the sway of the kingdom of Jesus Christ (cf. Amos 9:11–12 with Acts 15:16–17; Isa. 42:11; 60:1–9).[41]

Talking It Out

1. Abraham's decision to send his head servant on a mission to secure a wife for Isaac was directly dependent on the land promise that Yahweh had made to him so long before (Genesis 24:2–9). Why did Abraham lean on the land promise God had made? Base your answer on what you can discern from biblical text.

2. Abraham's servant asked God to confirm with a sign his answer to the servant's prayer (24:12–14), and God complied with the man's request (vv. 15–27). What do you think about asking God to indicate in some way his answer to one of your prayers? Do you think it's appropriate? Why or why not?

3. Often in Genesis, Moses simply tells what people do without explicitly saying that their words or deeds are right or wrong. And yet a careful reading of Genesis, as well as considering its stories in light of other biblical books, provides answers that help us discover what is actually moral and what is not. What can you conclude from this about how best to interpret the Bible, especially its accounts of historical persons and events?

LESSON 6

Like Father, Like Son

(25:19–26:33)

With the non-elect line covered, Moses returns to telling the story of the chosen line. Book 8, which covers significant events in Isaac's family history, starts in Genesis 25:19 and goes all the way through chapter 35. For the remainder of this lesson, we are going to look at Isaac's family story through Genesis 26 and then finish it up in the next two lessons.

Twins from a Barren Womb

Isaac and Rebekah did not have children right away. And the children they had brought a good deal of conflict into the family.

- *Compare the age of Isaac when he married Rebekah (25:20) with his age when his first sons were born (v. 26). How long did Isaac and Rebekah have to wait before they had children? What did it take for Rebekah's barrenness to be overcome (v. 21)?*

- *Yahweh had promised that Abraham's descendants would be plentiful (17:2–7) and that Isaac would be similarly blessed (v. 15–16, 19; 21:12). Why, then, do you suppose that it took so long for children to be added to Isaac's marriage? Was it only due to Rebekah's infertility?*

- *Rebekah experienced a troubling pregnancy. Why was this so, and what did Yahweh say about it (25:22–23)?*

- *What were the names given to Rebekah's twins, and what does each mean (vv. 24–26; see the study notes for these verses)?*

A Birthright Disdained

Like all children, even those within the same family, Jacob and Esau became their own persons, with their own likes and dislikes and character traits.

- *Summarize what 25:27 says about each son.*

- *Whom did Isaac favor, and whom did Rebekah (v. 28)?*

- *Read verses 29–34. What does this story reveal about each son? Be sure to consult the study note for verse 31 about the birthright in the ancient world. Also check out Hebrews 12:16.*

- *How did what Esau gave up prepare the way for him as the older brother to serve his younger brother (cf. Genesis 25:23)?*

- *If you grew up with other siblings or had some very close childhood friends, did you have the experience of so badly wanting something the other had that you were willing to exchange something that was yours in order to get it? Write about this event. Was the exchange worth the sacrifice you made?*

God Keeps His Word

Genesis 26 opens with a comparison between Abraham and Isaac, and the comparisons continue through most of the chapter. The similarities made between father and son are striking.

- *Read through Genesis 26:1–33. Outline the story below.*

- Now let's focus on the similarities and occasional differences between Abraham and Isaac by looking up the following passages in Genesis and next to each one filling in the appropriate details you find there.

Abraham's Experience	Isaac's Experience
12:10	*26:1*
12:11	*26:1–6*
12:11–14	*26:7*
12:15–20	*26:8–10*
13:2–10	*26:12–22*
13:14–17	*26:24*

13:18	26:25
14:17–24	26:26–31

The comparisons between Abraham and Isaac are meant to underscore that the divine promises and blessings made to the father were being passed down to his descendants. God was keeping his word.

Did you notice that when Abimelech, the king of Gerar, saw evidence that Rebekah was Isaac's wife and not his sister that the king issued a decree that anyone who laid a hand on Rebekah would face capital punishment (26:8–11)? This clearly shows that Isaac's attempted deception was completely unwarranted. Isaac and his wife would have been protected without the lie. They should have trusted in God and his promised blessing and not followed in the footsteps of Abraham when he schemed to protect himself and his wife in the earlier years of his walk with God.

EXPERIENCE GOD'S HEART

- *Sometimes it takes us a long time to fully trust God and his word. Can you recount a season in your life when your faith in God and his word was at a low ebb and you hatched your own plan to achieve something you wanted or protect something you had? Briefly describe what you did. Was it really necessary? Why or why not?*

- *List some of the promises God has made and how they have been fulfilled in your life.*

- *Now reflect on that list. Ask God to bring them to mind, especially when you feel yourself wondering if he keeps his word. Call on him to settle in your soul that he loves you and is always for you and that he keeps his word no matter what. Let his Spirit impress these truths on your mind and heart so you will always rely on them regardless of what fears and doubts you face.*

 THE BACKSTORY

The Abimelech and Phicol individuals who come up in Genesis 26 are probably not the same ones that Abraham dealt with. Ninety years separate Abraham's experience with Isaac's. While it's possible that the same king and military commander whom Abraham encountered were the ones Isaac faced, it's not likely. Abimelech may have been a title, such as Pharaoh and Caesar were. Part of the superscription of Psalm 34 provides the setting as the time when David "pretended to be insane before Abimelech" (NASB), an event described in 1 Samuel 21:10–15. There the king is referred to as "Achish king of Gath" (v. 10 NASB). So Achish was also known as Abimelech, indicating that Abimelech may have been one of his titles while Achish was his name. Similarly, Phicol may also be a title, but we have no evidence supporting this. It could also be as Ross suggests that "Phicol may simply be a namesake of the earlier Phicol" (Genesis 21:22, 32).[42]

With God a promise made is a promise kept. God kept his word to Abraham, and he kept it with Isaac. The physical progression toward the One who would defeat Satan continued. And this despite the fact that those in that chosen line didn't always believe or do what was right and wise. God's word doesn't depend on fallen creatures, whether they exercise faith or not. It only depends on him who is sovereign. But when his people truly rely on him, they learn more from him, enjoy his blessings more, and find greater satisfaction in life.

♥ SHARE GOD'S HEART

God is the Lord of history. Regardless how much world, national, and even family events seem out of control, we can rest assured that God continues to work out his plan for all creation, especially for his creatures who bear his image. Furthermore, as the apostle Paul says, we who are in Christ can rely on the fact that "every detail of our lives is continually woven together for good, for we are his [God's] lovers who have been called to fulfill his designed purpose" (Romans 8:28). This doesn't mean that every single thing that happens to us or within us is good. Rather, it means that God takes all that happens in our lives—whether good or evil—and works it out in such a way that it ultimately benefits us. That's how magnificent, wise, good, and powerful our Lord is.

God's sovereignty is a biblical teaching that we can comfort one another with. Paul used it to persuade the Christians in Rome that nothing could separate us from God's love and that this same God would ensure that all who are in Christ were on their way to becoming just like he who saved them (vv. 29–39).

- *Whom do you know who needs to be comforted with the truth of God's sovereignty? Take time to first pray for that person or persons. Then, with sensitivity to their situation and needs, share what you have learned about God's control over his world and his plan to work out all things for good, especially for those who have committed themselves to him.*

Talking It Out

1. Prayer and worship are recurring themes in this lesson and the previous one. Return to consider those passages and their contexts where these themes appear, and talk about what these practices accomplish and how you can better incorporate them into your life, your family's faith journey, and the activities of your church (see Genesis 24:12–15, 26–27, 42–45, 48, 52; 25:21; 26:25).

2. Yahweh appears three times in Genesis 25 and 26: once to Rebekah (25:22–23) and twice to Isaac (26:2–5, 23–24). What do you learn from these passages about the form of God's appearance (e.g., vision, dream, bodily manifestation, audible only)? Has he ever come to you in some way, or do you know someone to whom this has happened? Share your story and discuss what you learned through it about God and your relationship to him.

3. Read Hebrews 6:13–18. Add to that Titus 1:1–2. Reflect on those passages in relationship to the promises God made to Abraham, Sarah, and Isaac. The God who is truth will never lie. In fact, it is impossible for him to lie. We, on the other hand, can, like Abraham and Isaac, attempt to deceive. What do these facts about God and us tell you about his trustworthiness in comparison to ours? Who can you trust more? How does lying undermine trust? How does consistent truth-telling undergird trust?

LESSON 7

Jacob, Esau, and the Stolen Blessing

26:34–31:55

God's chosen are not sin-free, not in a fallen world. God had clearly selected through whom his conqueror would one day come, but his chosen man, Abraham, was far from perfect, as was his wife, Sarah. God kept his word to this couple; the promised son, Isaac, was born, married, and had children. Abraham's line was growing; divine blessing had shown itself certain. But because of the fallen human factor, the progress was messy. Polygamy rather than monogamy had entered into the process. The chosen seed had to be protected from the unchosen. Deceit had also marred even the lives of the faithful. And family members sometimes mistreated one another for selfish gain.

Still, God's plan kept moving forward. And those who recognized his presence and work often obeyed him, praised him, and worshiped him. God was achieving his goal one birth and one will at a time. But the human factor remained a challenge. The unfolding story of Isaac's family dramatically highlights these truths, all the while showing that the Sovereign God will always find a way to bless humankind no matter how difficult they make it.

Esau Marries Hittites

Although Esau was one of Isaac's sons, even the first born, he had already demonstrated that he was unfit for carrying on the chosen seed by selling his birthright for stew. Then, at forty years old, he took yet another clear step to show his disdain for his parents' wishes.

- *According to Genesis 26:34, what decision did Esau make?*

- *How did his decision affect his parents and the family dynamics (v. 35; see also the study note on this verse in TPT)?*

 THE BACKSTORY

The Hittites were one of the tribes that lived in the land of Canaan. They were descendants of Canaan, a son who came from Ham's line. Abraham had gone to great lengths to find a wife for Isaac outside of the land and peoples of Canaan (24:3–4), but Esau didn't share this desire or approach. Nor did he show any commitment to the marital ideal of monogamy (2:24). Esau seemed more interested in living life his way.

The result of Esau's marital choice led to misery for Isaac and Rebekah. The Hebrew words translated "made life miserable" (26:35) express intense anguish.[43] The same phrase describes Hannah's deep distress over her infertility (1 Samuel 1:10), and it's used by Job to express the bitterness and anguish he felt over his unjust suffering (Job 7:11; 10:1).

The Stolen Blessing

Esau, while an unfit and rebellious son, was still the one Isaac loved the most. And Jacob was the son most beloved by Rebekah. The sons' rivalry and the parents' differing favoritism collided when "Isaac was very old and blind" (Genesis 27:1).

- *Isaac called for Esau, and Esau came (27:1). What did Isaac say to his son (vv. 2–4)?*

- *Rebekah overheard Isaac's conversation with Esau (v. 5). What action did she take against Esau and for Jacob (vv. 5–13)?*

- Read verses 14–29 and answer the following questions.

What length did Rebekah go to deceive her husband (vv. 14–17)?

How many times did Jacob lie to his father about his identity, and what support did he offer that he was really Esau?

What was Isaac's blessing on the son he thought was Esau?

- Now read verses 30–46 and answer these questions.

Did Esau follow Isaac's instructions (vv. 30–31)?

Did Rebekah help Esau with the preparations for Isaac?

What happened when Isaac realized he had been tricked and Esau learned that Jacob had stolen what should have been his (vv. 32–38)?

What does Isaac eventually predict for the son he loved most (vv. 39–40)?

What is Esau's response to what Jacob had done (v. 41)?

Compare Esau's determination to murder his brother with what Cain (4:5–8) and Lamech did (4:23–24). Notice also what Jesus says about Satan and his seed (John 8:44; cf. Genesis 3:15). What does all of this reveal about Esau's heart at this time in his life?

What does Rebekah do to protect Jacob (Genesis 27:42–46)?

THE BACKSTORY

Isaac knew from what Yahweh had told Rebekah that their youngest son, Jacob, would one day be exalted over their eldest son, Esau (25:23). Esau and his descendants would serve Jacob and his, thereby making Jacob the recipient of the Abrahamic blessing (12:2–3; 17:4–7). But Isaac wanted Esau to have these benefits, hence the blessing he gave Jacob while thinking this son was Esau (27:27–29). Rebekah made sure that Jacob received what God had said he would, but rather than relying on God to handle the situation, she took matters into her own hands, and Jacob went along with her.

So Esau, instead of receiving his father's blessing, received an antiblessing from Isaac. As Waltke explains: "Esau inherits an antiblessing; he is denied both dominion over his brother and the earth's fertility (see 27:28–29; cf. Cain and Ishmael). This antiblessing is a parody on Jacob's blessing." Esau was twice told that he would live "far from" earth's and heaven's abundance (v. 39), while Jacob had been told that he would receive both (v. 28). Also, in Jacob's blessing, heaven is mentioned first and earth second, while in Esau's antiblessing, earth comes first and then heaven. Waltke says that this reversal is "a rhetorical device to signal and/or intensify the reversed blessing."[44]

Divinely speaking, Jacob receives what he should have, but he gets it by deception.

Humanly speaking, Esau is robbed of what Isaac wanted to give him, and the deceit involved goes back to Esau's mother and Isaac's wife—Rebekah. Imagine an adult son or daughter being plotted against by their mother. Or a husband being conned by his wife.

A messy situation indeed!

- *Before Jacob fled from Esau, what direction and blessing did Isaac give to his son (28:1–5)?*

- *How did Esau respond to his father's generosity toward Jacob (vv. 6–9)?*

- *Was Ishmael's side of the family, while not Canaanite, recipients of the Abrahamic blessing? What do you suppose this shows about Esau's assessment of his Hittite marriages?*

Jacob Commits to Yahweh

- *How old was Jacob when he left for Paddan-Aram (see TPT note on 28:5)?*

- *Read through 28:10–15. Describe Jacob's supernatural experience, especially what Yahweh told him.*

- *Then compare what Yahweh said to Jacob to the promises he made to Abraham in chapters 12 and 17. Is Yahweh passing along to Jacob the Abrahamic blessing?*

- *How does Jacob respond to Yahweh's revelation (28:16–22)?*

🐟 EXPERIENCE GOD'S HEART

Put yourself in Jacob's shoes. You are running from your brother after stealing a blessing from him. Your mother always supported you, but your father didn't until recently. You have never really been on good terms with your brother, and now he loathes you. You hope his anger against you will eventually dissipate, but you can't be certain of this. You are traveling to a land where you have never been and to a family you have not met. You set up camp and fall asleep after a very long day of travel. Then God comes to you in a dream, and rather than condemning you or correcting you, he blesses you with the first patriarch's blessing.

What would you do? How would you respond?

What does this tell you about God's amazing grace and mercy?

Has God dealt with you according to what you genuinely deserve? Or has he been gentle, kind, and abundantly gracious toward you?

Take some time now to ponder his dealings with you, and then respond to him with the gratitude, praise, and worship he so deserves.

Jacob Marries and Family Rivalry

- *Retell what happened when Jacob arrived somewhere near Haran (29:1–14). To gain more insight into this section of Scripture, refer to the study notes related to these verses.*

- *How would you describe Jacob's draw to Rachel?*

- *What deal did Jacob strike with Laban to win Rachel (vv. 15–19)?*

- *What was Jacob's experience like working for Laban (v. 20)?*

- *What happened after Jacob fulfilled his part of the agreement (vv. 21–30)?*

- *During this time, how did Leah fare as Jacob's wife (vv. 31–35)?*

🌑 SHARE GOD'S HEART

"When Yahweh saw that Leah was unloved, he opened her womb" (v. 31). This is just one of countless examples in Scripture that show God's heart for the unloved. When asked what the greatest commandments were, Jesus first mentioned loving God, and of the second he said, "You must love your friend [neighbor] in the same way you love yourself" (Matthew 22:39).

Whom do you know who is unloved or could use more love and care in their life? Reach out to them with the love God has for them. Think of some specific ways you can demonstrate his love. Love can come in so many forms: food, clothing, counsel, money, sharing the good news of redemption, caring conversation, transportation, home repairs and supplies, sharing heavy burdens, auto repairs...and the list goes on. Consider this person's situation and needs, then choose at least one way you can love them. You will be doing God's work in their life.

- *What action did Rachel take when she compared her infertility to her sister's reproductive success (Genesis 30:1–8)? Why did Rachel take this course?*

- *The rivalry continued between Rachel and Leah (vv. 9–24). Summarize what happened and why.*

- Under Rachel's name below, write down the names of the children she had, including the ones who came through her servant Bilhah. Under Leah's name, record the names of the children she had along with the ones conceived by her servant Zilpah.

    Rachel/Bilhah

    Leah/Zilpah

- *All of these children were Jacob's, and each (with the exception of the sole daughter, Dinah) became the founding ancestor of his own tribe. Together they comprised the twelve tribes of which nation (see 49:1–28)?*

THE BACKSTORY

Despite the competition, jealousy, and ill-conceived tactics of Rachel and Leah, their manipulations to bear children to Jacob do not turn out to be the deciding factor. The writer insists that it's Yahweh who first opens Leah's womb (29:31) and then Rachel's (30:22). The Lord is the one who exercises his sovereign choice, displaying his wisdom despite their foolishness, and his care and compassion for each woman regardless of their poor treatment of each other.

Jacob is not unsoiled either. He practices polygamy and discrimination between his wives. He never seems "to have forgiven [Leah] for consenting to deceive him" on what was to be his wedding night with Rachel. "He always regards Rachel as his wife and treats Leah and her children as inferior."[45] Moreover, Jacob "suffers divine discipline. As Jacob exploitatively 'exchanged' the birthright and blessing, Laban exchanges Jacob's wives, and Leah exchanges her marriage for a husband-for-hire."[46]

Still, God brings out of this family mess the ones who will generate the twelve tribes of Israel. And he "chose the despised mother, Leah, and exalted her to be the first mother. The kingly tribe of Judah and priestly tribe of Levi trace back to her, in spite of Jacob's love for Rachel and her son Joseph."[47] In fact, it will be through Leah and her son Judah that the Messiah would come (Luke 3:33; Matthew 1:2).

- Bow in silence before him who "causes everything to work together for the good of those who love [him] and are called according to his purpose for them" (Romans 8:28 NLT). Ponder what God is able to accomplish even through our messes. Then offer your thanksgiving to him, praising him for his goodness and abiding love for you.

Jacob's Last Dealings with Laban

In this next section of Genesis, Jacob, who had passively gone along with Laban, Rachel, and Leah, turns shrewd and aggressive. He hatches a plan to generate his own property since Laban had left him empty-handed and seemed content to keep him that way.

- *Genesis 30:25–43 tells the story of the deal struck between Jacob and Laban and how and why it worked out. Read through this passage and note below the key details of their agreement and what each man did to uphold or circumvent their agreement.*

- *Now read 31:1–16. This passage supplies the backstory, the rationale for the plan Jacob developed and carried out. Summarize what you learn.*

- *What were Jacob's departure plans, where did he and his family go, and what came with him without his knowledge (vv. 17–21)?*

- *What was the significance of Rachel's theft of the "household idols" (v. 19; see also TPT's study note on this verse)?*

- *How long did it take before Laban realized Jacob and his family were gone, and how long was it before he finally caught up to Jacob (vv. 22–23)?*

- *Summarize what happened just before Laban faced off with Jacob and then when the two men encountered each other (vv. 24–42).*

- *Laban and Jacob struck a parity covenant (an agreement between equals). What was its content? Whom did the men call on to be a witness of their agreement? What did they do to memorialize and seal their covenant (vv. 43–55)?*

Talking It Out

1. Has anyone ever taken advantage of you? How did that make you feel? Have you ever taken advantage of someone else, even defrauding them, such as what Jacob did to Esau? What was that experience like? How did you feel about yourself afterward? Discuss these experiences, knowing that none of us is pure and all of us are forgiven at the cross of Christ.

2. What was your home situation like growing up? Can you
   identify with the rivalries and favoritism that marked
   the home life of Jacob and Esau, including how those
   experiences rippled through their own families' lives?
   Generational sin is real, and it can be broken. Talk about
   your experience with generational sin and how you have
   tried to break the cycle. Remember, while God can bring
   good even out of our messes, he doesn't need our messes
   any more than we do. Life is always better when we live life
   his way rather than our own way.

3. Recall when "Rachel stole her father's household idols" (Genesis 31:19). She committed the first recorded act of godnapping! Now, only finite, puny, powerless gods can be ripped off from another human being. Could that ever happen to the God who created the entire universe from nothing? Could the same Yahweh who confused human language at Babel, who flooded the earth as judgment, and who opens and closes wombs be stolen and hidden away from view? Ponder how great Yahweh is. He has created us in his image; we dare not try to create him in ours. Praise him for who he is! And give thanks to him for loving you.

4. During their covenant making, Laban told Jacob, "Remember that even though no one else is with us, God is watching us" (Genesis 31:50). How true! The writer of Hebrews put God's omniscience this way: "There is not one person who can hide their thoughts from God, for nothing we do remains a secret, and nothing created is concealed, but everything is exposed and defenseless before his eyes, to whom we must render an account" (Hebrews 4:13). What do you find encouraging about this attribute of God? What about it is less than comforting? How should you live in light of it?

LESSON 8

Reconciliation, Revenge, and Renewal

(32:1–36:43)

The closer Jacob got to the area of Canaan where he was born, the closer he drew to Esau, the brother who had wanted to kill him. Would Esau still want revenge? God took steps to prepare Jacob for the meeting he feared.

- *Let's go back a bit to gain some context. Before Jacob encountered Laban many years before, whom did he face, and what did this supernatural figure tell him (Genesis 28:10–15)?*

- *What was Jacob's response to this divine encounter (vv. 20–22)?*

- *Now after Jacob left Laban, made a covenant with him, and then continued on his return to his homeland, who met him (32:1–2)?*

This angelic visitation displays God's protective presence to Jacob as he moves closer to Esau's home. It may also serve as a reminder to Jacob that he should fulfill his vow to God to worship him if he safely returns to his father's house (28:20–21).

- *What did Jacob do to pave the way to what he hoped would be a safe meeting with his brother (32:3–5)?*

- *What did Jacob's messengers tell him, and what decisions did Jacob make afterward (vv. 6–21)?*

- *One night, after Jacob sent away everyone who was with him along with all of his possessions, he was alone (vv. 22–24). During this time of solitude, he had a strange encounter with a God-man. Summarize what happened, including who initiated the event and what occurred afterward (vv. 24–31).*

- *Read through TPT's study notes on this encounter and write below what you learn about the significance of this event in Jacob's life.*

The Meeting

Jacob had wrestled with God, survived, and been blessed. He had even received a new name—Israel. He was now ready to face Esau and confront the deceit he had perpetrated against him.

- *Retell how Jacob chose to approach Esau (33:1–3).*

- *Describe the exchange between the two brothers (vv. 4–17). Does anything occur that surprises you? If so, what?*

- *Why do you think Jacob declined to travel with Esau and even left him going in the opposite direction?*

 SHARE GOD'S HEART

- *When Jacob faced Esau, he saw something in Esau that reminded him of God (v. 10). Have you ever encountered another person who reminded you of God in some significant way? Who was it, and what did this person say or do that reflected the Lord to you?*

- How do you reflect God to others? People need to know that he's real and loves them and knows how to help them mature and flourish. You may be the key to helping someone else encounter God in your likeness to him. Prayerfully contemplate how you do and can bear the image of God in a winsome way. Ask him to show you how you come across to others so you might better reveal his heart, especially to those who need him most.

Rape and Revenge

Jacob and his family eventually ended up just outside of "the Canaanite city of Shechem" (v. 18). Shechem was "about forty miles north of Jerusalem and [was] the site where Abram first built an altar in the promised land (see Gen. 12:7)."[48] Jacob purchased land there and set up an altar to Yahweh on the land (33:19–20).

- *A terrible sin was committed against Dinah, daughter of Leah and Jacob. What was it, who committed it, and what did the perpetrator's family hope to gain from it (34:1–12)?*

- *What was Jacob's response to the news of his daughter's rape (v. 5)?*

- *How did Dinah's brothers feel about what happened (v. 7)?*

- *How did Jacob's sons avenge the rape of their sister, and did their actions meet with their father's approval (vv. 13–31)?*

- *Compare Jacob's concerns over what his sons did and how his sons responded to him (vv. 30–31). What did Jacob fear and why? Who were his sons most concerned about and why?*

ⓗ WORD WEALTH

The story of Dinah's rape and how it was avenged is one of the most dramatic and disturbing accounts in Genesis. In telling it, Moses makes it clear that he finds the violation of Dinah not only immoral but also brutal (34:2). Consequently, his record of the brothers' outrage fits the crime (v. 7). At the same time, Moses also shows his disapproval of the brothers' plot of revenge. The Hebrew word translated "deceitfully" (v. 13) is *mirma*, which is used to describe "betrayal, deceit, or treachery." The word appears forty times in the Old Testament, and in each case its use indicates an indictment on the person who engages in *mirma* (e.g., see Genesis 27:35 and Jeremiah 5:27). According to Waltke's discussion of this word, "While deceit is expected by both parties in war, it is not acceptable in a peace treaty (cf. 2 Kings 9:23)." And *mirma* is not used in Scripture for "warfare situations. While the narrator approves of the brothers' moral indignation, he does not approve of their tactics."[49]

Bethel and Renewal

• *What action did God take after the events surrounding Dinah (35:1)?*

• *What was Jacob's response, and how did God protect him as he obeyed (vv. 2–5)?*

- *Once Jacob and all who were with him arrived in Bethel, what did Jacob build and why (vv. 6–7)?*

- *Genesis 35:9–15 records yet another appearance of God to Jacob. Summarize the encounter and what Jacob did right after it.*

 EXPERIENCE GOD'S HEART

Genesis records two previous appearances of God to Jacob (28:12–16; 32:30), one of which included an appearance to him in a dream. God's appearance to him, when he changed Jacob's name to Israel, marks the third divine encounter (35:9–15). This third time God confirmed what he had promised Jacob many years before in a dream, and he added one new promise—that kings would be in his line of descendants. God had made this same promise to Abraham (17:6). Yahweh wanted Jacob to know with certainty that he was in the chosen line and that his blessing was assured.

• *Record some truths and life direction that God has made known to you in such a way that you understand you can count on them.*

• *Now offer your thanksgiving to him for his assurances. He doesn't want you to doubt that he is for you—always!*

Rachel's End, Jacob's Sons, and Isaac's Death

On their journey from Bethel, Rachel went into labor.

• *How did the birth go, what was the son's name, and how did Jacob treat the death of the wife he loved the most (35:16–20)?*

- *After Rachel's death, Reuben, one of Leah's sons, sins. What does he do (v. 22)? Why might he have done this (see TPT study note on verse 22)?*

Genesis 35 closes with the names of Jacob's twelve sons, divided out according to who conceived them (vv. 22–26). From Jacob come the twelve sons from whom the twelve tribes of Israel (Jacob's new name) will derive. The chapter closes with Jacob finally returning to his father, Isaac. Although the text doesn't say this, the implication is that Jacob is reconciled to his father.

We're not told what the last days of Isaac were like, but we do learn how Moses summed up Isaac's life and portrayed his death and burial.

- *Verses 28–29 record Isaac's end. Summarize what you find there, including who buried him.*

- *What does the end of this chapter suggest about the relationship between Esau and Jacob?*

Esau's Family Line

Book 9 of Genesis consists of chapter 36, verses one through eight. It tells about Esau's family line in Canaan and his separation from that territory. This is the first generation of Esau's line. Book 10 goes from 36:10–43. It contains three sections. The first section concerns the sons and chiefs of Esau to the third generation (vv. 10–19). The second section lists Horite clans who lived in the land of Edom before Esau's arrival (vv. 20–30). The final section gives eight kings who reigned in Edom before any king arose in the established nation of Israel (vv. 31–43).

These two books wrap up Esau's role in Genesis. "As in the 'accounts' of Abraham's sons, the rejected line of Ishmael (25:12–18) is presented before the elect line of Isaac (25:19–35:29), so now in the 'accounts' of Isaac's sons, the rejected line of Esau (36:1–37:1) is presented before the elect line of Jacob (37:2–50:26)."[50] Esau did not have to end up this way in biblical history, as outside of the chosen line toward the Messiah. And although he was the son Isaac loved most, Esau never exhibited faith in the God Isaac served. He never built an altar to worship God, he disdained his birthright and exchanged it for stew, and he plotted murder against his brother. He also moved away from the promised land rather than settle in it. He failed to exhibit any signs of faith in Yahweh or his promises. Merrill Unger brings out Esau's true character and loss when he writes:

> Esau serves as a good illustration of the
> natural man of the earth (Heb. 12:16–17).
> In many respects a more honest man than
> Jacob, he was nevertheless destitute of
> faith. This was manifest in his despising
> the birthright because it was a spiritual
> thing, of value only as faith could see that
> value. The birthright involved the exercise
> of the priestly rights vested in the family
> head until the establishment of the Aaronic

priesthood. The Edenic promise of one who would "bruise" Satan was fixed in the family of Abraham (Gen. 3:15); the order of promise was Abel, Seth, Shem, Abraham, Isaac, *Esau*. As the firstborn Esau was in the distinct line of the promise to Abraham: "and in you all the families of the earth shall be blessed" (12:3). For all that was revealed, these great messianic promises might have been realized in Esau. For a fleeting, fleshly gratification Esau sold this birthright. Although Jacob's understanding of the birthright at the time was undoubtedly carnal and faulty, his desire for it, nevertheless, evidenced true faith.[51]

Now let's look at some of the details of this genealogical table.

- *By what other name was Esau known (Genesis 36:1; cf. 25:30)? His brother Jacob also received the name of what would become a nation. What was that name (35:10)? Compare this transformation of personal names into national names with 25:23. What has happened?*

Genesis 36:2–3 gives the names of three Canaanite wives, and two of them don't match up to the wives named in 26:34 and 28:9. Perhaps the earlier named wives had died, or two of them had taken different names, or maybe Esau had six wives and the ones listed in chapter 36 were the ones he favored.[52]

- *Where were the children of these Canaanite wives born (36:4–5)? Where did Esau then travel and settle and why (vv. 6–8)?*

- *Was Esau's reason for leaving the promised land for Seir really justified? Reflect on what Hamor said about Jacob and his family and possessions in 34:21. Also compare Esau's rationale to Lot's (13:5–6, 11–12). What did you learn about the amount of available space in Canaan?*

The next section of Genesis 36 focuses on Esau's grandsons and the tribes that descended from his sons. The interest of these ancestral details is to show the development of "the Edomites in the hill country of Seir" (v. 9).

- *How many sons came from Eliphaz, the son of Esau's wife Adah (vv. 10–13)?*

- *Reuel, who was the son of Esau's wife Basemath, had how many sons (vv. 10–13)?*

- *How many sons did Esau's wife Oholibamah have (v. 14)?*

- *Now under each wife/son above, specify the number of tribes that descended from each (vv. 15–18).*

Genesis 36:20–30 gives the names of "the tribes [that] descended from Seir the Horite, of the original inhabitants of Edom" (v. 20). Esau destroyed them (Deuteronomy 2:22) while marrying at least one of them. Let's see whom he married.

- *Compare Genesis 36:3 with verse 25. Whose name appears in both verses?*

The last section in this genealogical chapter lists "eight kings who reigned in Edom" (Genesis 36:31). King Hadad is highlighted as the one who "defeated the Midianites in the land of Moab" (v. 35). Later in history, the first king of Israel, Saul, would wage war against Edom, seeing the Edomites as enemies of Israel (1 Samuel 14:47). When David became Israel's king, he subjugated the Edomites under his rule and placed garrisons throughout their land (2 Samuel 8:14; 1 Kings 11:15–16). The nation of Israel (Jacob) had become greater than the nation of Edom (Esau).

Talking It Out

1. Jacob physically wrestled with God, and we often wrestle with him spiritually. We don't understand what he's doing and why. We're confused, hurt, angry, or impatient. *What is God waiting for? Why won't he answer? Why is he permitting me to go through this hard situation?* Reflect on God's ways with you and with others you know. Discuss those with someone whom you know will be a trusted confidant for you. God is always faithful, but his timetable is usually not ours, and his ways are always higher and greater than ours. What can you do to wrestle with him less and trust in him more?

2. Jacob and Esau reconciled, but that didn't require that they live close together. What about their reconciliation did you find unexpected? Have you ever experienced reconciliation with a family member, friend, or work associate? What happened? What did you learn about reconciliation through the experience?

3. Dinah's brothers engaged in deceit and slaughter to avenge the sexual assault of their sister. What do you think about what they did? If you find their actions wrong or over the top, what do you think they should have done and why?

LESSON 9

Joseph, Betrayal, and Transformation

(37:1–38:30)

Jesus once said, "What appears humanly impossible is more than possible with God. For God can do what man cannot" (Luke 18:27). Over and over in Genesis, we have seen God do what no human being can. He creates the universe from nothing; we cannot make anything from nothing. He creates and gives life; we procreate through the process he has already made possible. He makes us his image bearers; we duplicate his work through procreation. He covers the globe with water; we sometimes find ourselves in the position of having to fight back the waters so we can live.

God is God, and we are not. What good we have ultimately came from him. We work with what he has provided for us. Even our abilities to reason, to feel, to love, to choose, to reproduce, to work, to worship...all find their source in him. We can use them to go astray from his will, but we cannot remove ourselves from his sovereign charge.

The final chapters of Genesis drive these facts home. God does the humanly impossible, and he does it through one of Israel's sons, Joseph. Joseph's trust in God and obedience to him become God's chosen means to turn disaster into blessing, not just for his chosen line but for the nations. Yahweh keeps his covenant with

Abraham, Isaac, and Jacob, and he does it through the messiness of human history.

Dreams and Deceit

The setting for the start of Joseph's story is "the land of Canaan" (Genesis 37:1), the promised land. He is with his father, Jacob, the third patriarch who is now called Israel after the nation still to come. J. Barton Payne dates this time period in Joseph's life, from his birth to his later teenage years, from 1915 to 1898 BCE.[53] Book 11 of Genesis begins here: "This is the story of the family [*toledot*] of Jacob." This is the last family history in Genesis.

- *How old was Joseph at this time, whom did he serve, and what was the family's livelihood (37:2)?*

- *How old was Israel around this time (see TPT note on 37:1–2)?*

- *What set Joseph apart from his brothers, and how did they regard him because of it (vv. 2–4; see also TPT notes on these verses)?*

- *Joseph had two dreams, both of which he shared with his family. What were the dreams, what interpretations did his family give to those dreams, and how did his brothers and father respond to them (vv. 5–11)?*

- *Why do you think Israel "kept pondering Joseph's dream" (v. 11)? What had happened in his life to make him more curious and sensitive toward dreams?*

 THE BACKSTORY

Favoritism has played a negative role many times in Jacob's family history. In 37:3 we're told that "Israel's love for Joseph surpassed that for his other sons." Recall that

> Isaac loved Esau more than Jacob, Rebekah
> loved Jacob more than Esau, and...Jacob
> loved Rachel more than Leah (25:28;
> 29:30). [Jacob's] old love for Rachel is
> now transferred to Joseph, Rachel's son.
> It is therefore hardly surprising that "they
> [Joseph's brothers] hated him," but that
> it is said three times (vv. 4, 5, 8) indicates
> the intensity of their feelings. Once again,
> parental attitudes are emerging in the
> children. Leah is twice described as "hated,"
> so in turn her sons "hate" (29:31, 33).[54]

 SHARE GOD'S HEART

- *Did favoritism play a role in your family when you were growing up? Do you play favorites in your home life? If your answer is yes to either question, how has favoritism worked out? What has been its consequences?*

- *If favoritism has not been present in your family life, why do you think that is?*

- *What can you do to show God's faithful, sacrificial love to all your family members, thereby overcoming favoritism by showing a better way to do and be good?*

The next scene begins the transition from the Hebron valley to the city of Shechem, the place where Dinah had been raped two years before (37:12, 14). Joseph would have been fifteen at that time. Israel wants Joseph to travel to Shechem to check on his brothers there who are caring for "their father's flock" (vv. 12–14). The distance between Hebron and Shechem was about fifty miles, so it was not a short errand.[55]

- *What happened when Joseph initially arrived at Shechem (vv. 14–17)? How much farther did he have to travel (see TPT study note 'c' on v. 17)?*

- *As Joseph drew within eyesight of his brothers, what had they plotted to do to him and why (vv. 18–20)?*

- *What was Reuben's counter suggestion, and why did he make it (vv. 21–22)?*

- *What did his brothers end up doing against Joseph, and why did they change their plan yet again (vv. 23–28)?*

Reuben must have been away part of the time because he was grief-stricken when he found Joseph gone from the pit (v. 29).

- *What did Reuben then do, and what cover-up did the brothers concoct (vv. 30–32)?*

- *How did Jacob handle the news of his missing son (vv. 33–35)?*

- *Where did Joseph finally end up (v. 36)?*

Judah's Family Troubles

Before Joseph's situation in Egypt develops, Moses turns to focus on Judah—the brother who suggested that Joseph be sold to traders (37:26–27). Judah was "the fourth son of Jacob and Leah, and whole brother to Reuben, Simeon, and Levi, older than himself, and Issachar and Zebulun, who were younger (Gen. 29:35)." Judah was born around 1950 BCE.[56] Genesis 38 is dedicated to telling a part of Judah's story after Joseph is sold into Egyptian bondage. According to Bible scholar Derek Kidner:

> As a piece of family history this chapter is
> important in settling the seniority within
> the tribe of Judah, and it contributes to the
> royal genealogy in Matthew 1:3; Luke 3:3.
> As a rude interruption of the Joseph story

it serves other purposes as well. It creates suspense for the reader, with Joseph's future in the balance; it puts the faith and chastity of Joseph, soon to be described, in a context which sets off their rarity; and it fills out the portrait of the effective leader among the ten brothers.[57]

With Joseph gone and Israel believing his youngest son was dead, Judah "left his brothers at Hebron and went to Adullam to stay with a man named Hirah" (Genesis 38:1).

- *How far was Adullam from Hebron (see TPT study note for Genesis 38:1)? What did Judah do in that city and then later in Chezib (vv. 2–5)?*

- *When Judah's sons were grown, he arranged for Er, his oldest son, to marry Tamar. How did that work out (vv. 6–7)?*

- *Judah then had Tamar marry whom, and what happened in that marriage (vv. 8–10)?*

- *With two sons now deceased, what decision did Judah make to protect his third son, Shelah (v. 11)?*

- *Judah's daughter-in-law, Tamar, decided to take her future into her own hands. What plot did she hatch, and how did it work out (vv. 12–26)?*

- *What was Judah's final verdict on what Tamar had done (v. 26)? Do you agree with his conclusion and action? Explain your answer.*

- *How many children did Tamar have, and what were their names (vv. 27–30)?*

Among Tamar's children, the younger prevailed over the older in birth. Many years earlier, the younger Jacob also won the rivalry with his older brother Esau; it just took longer.

 THE BACKSTORY

Judah's story depicts the start of his change of character. In the end, he accepts blame for what he did to Tamar. Later in Genesis, he plays an important protector role for his brothers and father. Judah transforms into a different kind of a man.

And what about Tamar? She was a Canaanite, outside of the chosen line, not a part of the Abrahamic covenant at all. And yet, she shows more commitment to having children in Judah's family than his sons do.

Despite the deaths of her first two husbands, she [Tamar] is anxious to marry Shelah. And when she is thwarted by her father-in-law, she manages to find a way of having children through him. Such determination to propagate descendants of Abraham, especially by a Canaanite woman, is remarkable, and so despite her foreign background and irregular behavior, Tamar emerges as the heroine of this story. She is like Melchizedek (chap. 14) and [Abimelech] (chap. 26), one of those foreigners who see God's hand at work in Abraham and his descendants and therefore align themselves with Israel.[58]

❤ EXPERIENCE GOD'S HEART

God loves us as we are, but he also loves us so much that he won't leave us as we are. If we remain tender toward the work of his Spirit, we will undergo life-changes in our character, decisions, and rest of our ways. Even when we blow it, like Judah, we'll accept responsibility for our actions and do what we can to make things right.

- *Have you recently made an error in judgment that you have not owned up to? If so, consider what you can do to set things right.*

Talking It Out

1. Family life can be tough sometimes, even traumatic. Whether one family member or more bring trouble into the family or it comes from the outside, family is not always the safe haven it was meant to be. Talk about some of your family experiences. And when appropriate, relate them to Joseph's family life. What do you have in common with his family? How does your experience differ? How have you dealt with family relationships that are not the way they were supposed to be?

2. Have you ever felt desperation close to what Tamar felt? What did it concern? What did you do about it? What did you learn about yourself and God through it?

3. God reveals his will to us in a wide variety of ways. In this section of Genesis, dreams were the primary means. How has God made his will known to you? Discuss the different ways God manifests his presence and plan. Allow this discussion to expand your ideas about how God communicates and how effective those methods are in human lives.

LESSON 10

Joseph's First Years in Egypt

(39:1–41:46)

With Judah's story told, Moses returns to Joseph, taking up his story in the foreign land of Egypt. It begins with involuntary servitude, and Payne puts the years for this between 1898 and 1885 BCE.[59]

Serving Potiphar

• *Who purchased Joseph from the Ishmaelite traders, and what was this man's position under Pharaoh (Genesis 39:1)?*

• *Read 39:2–6. How many times does the text say that Yahweh was with Joseph and blessing him? What specifically did Yahweh do for Israel's son?*

 EXPERIENCE GOD'S HEART

Although Joseph had no choice in his work for Potiphar, Joseph still worked to serve him so he and his household would flourish. Joseph was so successful that even the Egyptian Potiphar realized that Yahweh was blessing Joseph and that he could relax and enjoy life with Joseph in charge.

- *What kind of worker are you? Whether you are an employer or an employee, no matter your position or level of responsibility, are you someone people can depend on? Can they rest in you, or do they worry about you? If the former, why is that so? If the latter, why do you make them anxious?*

- *How can you experience God's blessing on your work? If you're not sure, ask God to show you. Also seek out a godly man or woman whom you can talk to about this. Lay out a plan based on what you learn that will help you mature into the kind of worker people can rely on.*

From Trusted to Dismissed

- *Potiphar's wife was attracted to Joseph. Why? And what did she want Joseph to do with her (vv. 6–7)?*

- *How did Joseph handle her advances and why (vv. 8–10)?*

- *How did Potiphar's wife get Joseph in trouble with her husband (vv. 11–18)?*

- *Was her deception effective? What happened to Joseph (vv. 19–20)?*

Serving the Warden

- *How does Joseph handle prison life, and what does Yahweh do for him (vv. 21–23)?*

Interpreting Dreams in Prison

When Genesis 40 opens, "Eleven years had passed since the time Joseph was sold into slavery. He was about twenty-eight at this time."[60]

- *What happened before Pharaoh that increased the prison population under Potiphar by two? Who were the new prisoners, and under whose charge were they placed (40:1–4)?*

- *Pharaoh's ex-steward and ex-baker had dreams while in prison that they couldn't interpret (vv. 5–8). Whom did Joseph tell them could explain the meaning of their dreams, what was each man's dream, and what was the interpretation of each (vv. 8–19)?*

- *Did Joseph's interpretation of each man's dream prove to be accurate (vv. 20–22)? Did these events bring about a change in Joseph's situation (v. 23)?*

Pharaoh's Dreams

Two more years in prison passed for Joseph. He had been incarcerated unjustly and then forgotten by one of the prisoners he helped. He remained in prison, still flourishing due to God's blessing but serving time, nonetheless.

• *Around this time, Pharaoh dreamed twice in the same night. Describe each dream (41:1–7).*

• *What effect did these dreams have on Pharaoh, and to whom did he first go in his search for an interpreter (v. 8)?*

• *Who finally told Pharaoh about Joseph, and what did he say about this prisoner (vv. 9–13)?*

- *What did Pharaoh then do (vv. 14–24)?*

- *What was Joseph's interpretation of Pharaoh's dreams (vv. 25–32)?*

- *What counsel did Joseph give Pharaoh as a result of the dreams' interpretation (vv. 33–36)?*

Serving Pharaoh

• *How did Pharaoh and his advisers respond to Joseph's counsel (vv. 37–40)?*

• *What else did Pharaoh do to display his confidence in Joseph (vv. 41–45)?*

• *How old was Joseph when he became the second in command in all of Egypt, and how extensively could he exercise his freedom (v. 46)?*

 THE BACKSTORY

Among Pharaoh's gifts to Joseph was an Egyptian wife who was "the daughter of Potiphera" (41:45). The name of her father, Potiphera, means "he whom Re (the sun-god) has given." He was "the priest of Heliopolis" (v. 45), a city that was "ten miles north-east of Cairo and was the center of Egyptian sun worship."[61] His daughter's name, Asenath (v. 45), means "belonging to (the goddess) Neith."[62] Joseph's marriage into this priestly family secured his political promotion.

Pharaoh also gave Joseph a new name: Zaphenath-Paneah, or Revealer of Secrets (v. 45). Pharaoh's renaming Joseph "symbolizes Joseph's new identity, validates Joseph's Egyptian position, and signifies Pharaoh's greater authority (i.e., only he has the power to name Joseph). Joseph is no longer an Asiatic slave but an Egyptian vizier."[63]

💚 SHARE GOD'S HEART

Before his time in Egypt, Joseph seemed more interested in getting his brothers in trouble rather than working with them and serving them. But his brothers' betrayal and his trials in Egypt changed him. He faithfully served God, Potiphar, fellow inmates, Pharaoh, and then the Egyptian people. His heart changed. He became other-centered rather than self-centered. He worked to exalt others instead of himself. He served, even when his service went unrewarded.

> • *Is this your heart in respect to others? Do you seek to serve those around you, to care for them, and to put them before yourself? If so, in what ways do you carry this out? If not, what can you put into practice even this week to begin to seek the welfare of others more than your own?*

Joseph went from hated brother to highly respected and trusted servant to Pharaoh. He went from being in command of nothing to being second in command over all of Egypt. He went from prisoner to reigning government official. What we don't yet know is what happened between him and his family in Canaan. Do they reconnect? If so, how? And when they do, will Joseph exact revenge for what his brothers did to him? The remainder of Genesis tells the story.

Talking It Out

1. Have you ever done something to help another person only to have that person ignore your contribution and perhaps turn their back on you? What happened? How did you respond to this person? What did you learn through the situation?

2. While others hurt Joseph and took advantage of him, God did not. Yahweh honored Joseph's faithfulness and then, in his time, exalted him to the position and role he wanted Joseph to play. Are you patient, willing to wait on God to exalt you rather than trying to do that yourself? What are some of the advantages to permitting others to see your value instead of pointing that out to them?

3. Not every believer is meant to lead in such a visible and exalted way as Joseph did, but all of us will be leaders—influencers—at various times in our lives. How has God been preparing you for what he has planned? Even if you don't know what he's directing you to, you can grasp what he has been teaching you. This instruction is his preparation work for this life and beyond. What are you learning?

LESSON 11

Joseph, Provider to Nations

(41:47–47:27)

Psalm 105 contains a stirring poetic commentary on God and his faithfulness, especially as it concerns his dealings with his chosen people. Notice the references to Genesis:

> Though a thousand generations may pass away,
> he [God] is still true to his word.
> He has kept every promise he made to Abraham
>   and to Isaac.
> His promises have become an everlasting covenant
>   to Jacob,
> as a decree to Jacob.
> He said to them, "I will give you all the land of
>   Canaan
> as your inheritance."
> They were very few in number when God gave
>   them that promise,
> and they were all foreigners to that land.
> They were wandering from one land to another
> and from one kingdom to another.
> Yet God would not permit anyone to touch them,
> punishing even kings who came against them.
> He said to them, "Don't you dare lay a hand on my
>   anointed ones,

and don't do a thing to hurt my prophets!"
So God decreed a famine upon Canaan-land,
cutting off their food supply.
But he had already sent a man ahead of his people
   to Egypt;
it was Joseph, who was sold as a slave.
His feet were bruised by strong shackles
and his soul was held by iron.
God's promise to Joseph purged his character
until it was time for his dreams to come true.
Eventually, the king of Egypt sent for him, setting
   him free at last.
Then Joseph was put in charge of everything under
   the king;
he became the master of the palace
over all the royal possessions.
Pharaoh gave him authority over all the princes of
   the land,
and Joseph became the teacher of wisdom to the
   king's advisers. (Psalm 105:8–22)

In the closing chapters of Genesis, Joseph is just under Pharaoh in authority over Egypt. Joseph, once the slave of Potiphar and then servant to the prison warden, is carrying out his plan to prepare Egypt for the great famine to come. All of Egypt's other government officials and people must comply with Joseph's orders and direction. If they don't, they must answer to him and even to Pharaoh himself. That's great power!

But high position and extensive authority have come to Joseph because Pharaoh recognized in him someone greater than either of them—God. Pharaoh certainly didn't know God as Joseph did, and he likely thought of God differently from how Joseph knew him. Still, this ruler of Egypt put his full trust in Joseph (Genesis 41:38–44) because he saw God at work in this foreigner.

In this lesson, we learn how Joseph carried out the authority entrusted to him and how God worked through him to save his family, the chosen line, Egypt, and the rest of the nations.

From Abundance to Famine

Payne puts the years of Joseph's powerful role in Egypt from 1885 to 1805 BCE, with the closing year as the time of his death.[64] If this is the case, then Joseph held his position through the reigns of five pharaohs, all rulers during Egypt's Middle Kingdom: Senusret II (1897–1878), Senusret III (1878–1860), Amenemhat III (1860–1815), Amenemhat IV (1815–1807), and Sobekneferu, sister to Amenemhat IV (1807–1802).[65] Joseph began his political position at age thirty and apparently held it until his death at age one hundred ten (Genesis 41:46; 50:22, 26).

- *What does it suggest about Joseph that he maintained his high position in Egypt through the administrations of five pharaohs?*

- *Joseph put his prophetic knowledge and plan into practice. What did that look like during the seven years of bumper crops (41:47–49)?*

- *Joseph's marriage produced children during this time. What names did they receive, and how did their names reflect Joseph's Egyptian experience and his faith in God (vv. 50–52; also see TPT study notes for these verses)?*

- *What happened when the seven years of abundance came to an end (vv. 53–57)?*

- *What indications do you have in the text that the famine was severe? Would you say that what happened in Egypt vindicated Joseph's interpretation of Pharaoh's dreams?*

☻ EXPERIENCE GOD'S HEART

Among the certainties of human life on earth is that tough times will come. Sometimes we can glean that they are coming, and occasionally God gives us a heads up. Most of the time, however, we need to do what we can to prepare for life's jolts. And prepared or not, we need to rely on him who is sovereign over human history and who loves us to see us through whatever tough times come our way.

- *What uncertainties have you prepared for?*

- *What are some steps you can begin to take to prepare for the down times sure to come?*

From Canaan to Egypt

The story now shifts from Egypt to Canaan, from the younger brother to the many older brothers, from the son supposedly lost and dead to the rest of the family living under famine in the promised land.

- *Who in the family first learns about the availability of food in Egypt, and what does he do about it (42:1–5)?*

- *To whom do the brothers have to appear, and how do they show their respect (v. 6)?*

- *Compare the brothers' actions before Joseph to one of his earlier dreams (37:5–8). Did this dream come true?*

- *How does Joseph respond to them (42:7–17)?*

- *What are the conditions of Joseph's test (vv. 18–20)?*

- *After they heard the test's terms, the brothers spoke among themselves. How did they interpret what was happening to them? What do you learn about their earlier treatment of Joseph (vv. 21–22)?*

- *What was Joseph's response to his brothers' comments (vv. 23–26)?*

Shock and Fear

- *Now on their way back to Canaan, what do the brothers discover, and how does it affect them (vv. 27–29)?*

- *Once they arrive home and come before their father, Israel, what happens (vv. 30–38)?*

Return to Egypt

There were no more trips back to Egypt for a while. Israel had chosen to hold out, probably hoping the famine would come to an end, thereby making more journeys to Egypt unnecessary.

- *What took place that changed the father's mind (43:1–2)?*

- *Describe the exchange between Israel and his sons over the return trip. Focus especially on Judah's role in the discussion and what Israel finally decides (vv. 3–15).*

- When the brothers, with Benjamin with them, appear again before Joseph in Egypt, what happens? Use the following story list to help you organize the flow of events:

  Joseph tells his chief servant to (vv. 16–17)...

  His brothers are fearful because (v. 18)...

  His brothers interact with the chief servant and (vv. 19–25)...

  After Joseph returns home (vv. 26–34)...

Another Test of Brothers

With everyone full of food and drink in the midst of a raging famine, Joseph creates yet another test of his brothers' love and loyalty.

- *What does Joseph do (44:1–5)?*

 THE BACKSTORY

The silver goblet placed in one of the sacks taken by Joseph's brothers was significant to Egyptian religious practice. It was used in divination "to discover secrets hidden from men" (44:5). As Waltke explains:

> The techniques of hydromancy (pouring water into oil), oelomancy (oil into water), and oenomancy (wine into another liquid) were commonplace in the ancient Near East. Through the surface patterns formed by pouring one type of liquid upon another, the practitioner professed to determine the mind of the gods with reference to the future, to the source of trouble, or to the truth of guilt or innocence. Referring to the wine goblet as a divining cup contributes to the ruse. Joseph receives revelation from God alone (37:5–9; 41:16...).[66]

Joseph wanted to raise to a higher level the gravity of his brothers' alleged crime while maintaining the ruse of his identity as an Egyptian official. The subterfuge worked.

- *When Joseph's chief servant confronts the brothers, what happens (44:6–13)?*

- *When the brothers faced Joseph again, what did Joseph say to them (vv. 14–15)?*

- *An exchange occurred between Joseph and Judah. Summarize what each man said, including the sacrifice Judah was willing to make for Benjamin and Israel (vv. 16–34).*

🌙 SHARE GOD'S HEART

God's love is sacrificial, even to the point of his Son going to the cross for us to make it possible for us to receive his payment for our sins and thereby become reconciled to God and live forever in him (Galatians 3:20). Because "Jesus sacrificed his life for us...we should be willing to lay down our lives for one another" (1 John 3:16). This doesn't just mean giving up our lives for others. It also means giving others what they need when we have the means to meet their need. As the apostle John says, "If anyone sees a fellow believer in need and has the means to help him, yet shows no pity and closes his heart against him, how is it even possible that God's love lives in him?" (v. 17). Our lives must "demonstrate love in action" (v. 19).

Judah showed his love through his willingness to make personal sacrifices for his father's sake and Benjamin's.

• *To whom can you demonstrate your love this week?*

• *What is this person's need, and what can you do to meet it?*

- *If you aren't sure what to do, let the God who is love reveal that to you. Commit this person and situation to prayer and then remain receptive to what God shows you that he wants you to do.*

Brotherly Revelation

- *Describe Joseph's revelation of himself to his brothers, especially what he came to believe about why he ended up in Egypt (Genesis 45:1–8).*

- *What did Joseph now want his brothers to do (vv. 9–13)?*

- *Describe the rest of their encounter (vv. 14–15).*

- *What was Pharaoh's response to Joseph's reunion with his brothers (vv. 16–20)?*

- *When the brothers left Egypt for Canaan, what did they take with them (vv. 21–24)?*

Family Reunion in a Foreign Land

- *After the brothers returned to their father in Canaan, how did Israel respond to their great news (vv. 25–28)?*

- *On their return trip to Egypt, Israel and his family first stopped in Beersheba. How old was Israel at this point, and what happened at their camping site (46:1–4; consult the note on v. 2)?*

- *When they left for Egypt, what and whom did they take (46:5–7)?*

Before the writer describes what happened when Israel and his family reunited with Joseph in Egypt, he provides a genealogical list of Israel's family—the ones who went into the foreign land knowing that this was God's will and that one day he would bring back their descendants into the promised land (vv. 8–25).

- What was the total number of Israel's direct descendants, excluding their wives (v. 26)?

- When Joseph's sons and their wives are added, what did the total number come to (v. 27)?

- When they arrived in Egypt, whom did Israel send to Joseph to guide the large entourage into Goshen (v. 28)?

- *Describe the family reunion with Joseph and what he did to prepare them to meet Pharaoh (vv. 29–34).*

 # THE BACKSTORY

Wenham provides some insight into the reference to seventy of Israel's family going to Egypt: "That Jacob went down to Egypt with seventy persons is mentioned in Exod 1:5; Deut 10:22. Often seventy seems a round number for a large group or family (Exod 24:1, 9; Judg 8:30; 12:14), and Gen 10 records that seventy nations were descended from Noah. Thus the nation of Israel represents the family of man in microcosm."[67]

Israel before Pharaoh

- *As you read the account of Israel and his brothers finally coming before the supreme ruler of ancient Egypt, picture the scene (Genesis 47:1–10). Also revisit Joseph's second dream—the one he shared with his brothers before they sold him into bondage (37:9–10). Below jot down what strikes you about this encounter and how it fulfills Joseph's dream. Keep in mind all the events that led up to this moment, including the famine still worsening in Egypt and beyond.*

- *With Pharaoh's direction and blessing, what does Joseph do for his father and family (47:11–12)?*

Egypt Grows Rich

While the famine rages and worsens, Egypt grows rich because of Joseph's plan and policies. He goes through a process that gradually brings everyone's livestock and land into Pharaoh's possession and turns almost all the Egyptians into serfs. And all of this happens voluntarily!

- Read 47:13–26 and answer the questions that follow:

    What steps led to the complete takeover of everyone's livestock and land?

    As serfs now working Pharaoh's land, how much of what they produced had to be delivered to Pharaoh?

    Who was exempt from all of this and why?

- *How did Israel and his descendants fare during this time (v. 27)?*

Talking It Out

1. Israel and his family receive shocking news at various times in this part of Joseph's story. What are some alarming reports your family has received? How did your family handle the news? What has been some of the fallout?

2. Several times we're told that Joseph wept, sometimes over gain and other times over loss. When have you cried? What did weeping do for you? Did others comfort you or rejoice with you? Did you experience God at all through your tears? If so, how?

3. Through Joseph, God took care of the chosen line and all the peoples and nations affected by the great famine, including Egypt. Discuss what this reveals about God, his love, the trustworthiness of his promises, and his involvement in human history. Also consider what he can do through the faithfulness of even a single individual.

LESSON 12

End of an Era

(47:28–50:26)

Israel knew he was nearing death, so he began to get his affairs in order. First on his list was making a request of Joseph.

- *How old was Israel at this time (Genesis 47:28)?*

- *What did he ask of Joseph, and did Joseph say he would comply? Then whom did Israel turn to (vv. 29–31)?*

The next thing Israel did was sparked by a visit from Joseph, who brought his sons with him (48:1).

- How did Israel respond to Joseph and his sons' visit
  (48:2–11)?

- When Joseph placed his sons before Israel, what did his
  father do that was so odd, and why did he say he chose
  to bless the sons this way (vv. 12–14, 17–19)?

- What was Israel's blessing on both sons (vv. 15–16, 20)?

- What was the consequence of Israel's arm crossing (v. 20)?

Yet another thing Israel did before he died was to give Joseph something more than his brothers.

- *What did he promise Joseph (vv. 21–22; see also TPT study note 'a' for v. 22)?*

While on his deathbed, Israel had all of his sons come around him so he could give each one a prophetic pronouncement about their future (49:1–2).

- Next to each son's name below, summarize the prophecy Israel made. Be sure to consult the study notes for each prophecy to gain more clarity and background on each pronouncement.

Reuben (49:3–4):

Simeon and Levi (vv. 5–7):

Judah (vv. 8–12):

Zebulun (v. 13):

Issachar (vv. 14–15):

Dan (vv. 16–17):

Gad (v. 19):

Asher (v. 20):

Naphtali (v. 21):

Joseph (vv. 22–26):

Benjamin (v. 27):

- *In the middle of these prophecies, Israel broke out in prayer (v. 18). What did he say, and what was its significance? See also TPT study note 'b' for verse 18.*

Each son would head up his own tribe. Together, they began "the twelve tribes of Israel" (v. 28).

Israel's Death and Funeral

The rest of Genesis 49 presents Israel's last words to his sons and his death.

- *What did Israel ask his sons to do for him (vv. 29–32)?*

- *How did Israel die (v. 33)?*

- *How did Joseph respond to his father's death (50:1–3)?*

After the mourning period of seventy days was over (50:4), Joseph approached Pharaoh with a request.

- *What did Joseph ask Pharaoh, and did Pharaoh grant his request (vv. 4–6)?*

- *Who and what accompanied Joseph to Canaan to bury Israel (vv. 7–9)?*

- *What happened when this huge procession reached "the threshing floor of Atad" (vv. 10–11)?*

• *Was Israel's burial request fulfilled (vv. 12–13)?*

DIGGING DEEPER

Several times from the account of Abraham through Israel, the text mentions joining one's ancestors after death. Look up the passages listed in the chart below and fill in the other columns. For the speaker or narrator, name who's talking. The recipient will be who is spoken to or about. And what's said concerns comments about ancestors.

Joining One's Ancestors

Genesis Passage	The Speaker or Narrator	The Recipient	What's Said
15:15			
25:8			
25:18			
35:29			
48:21			
49:29			

- *What do you conclude about who the ancestors were and whether they were still living or dead?*

- *Do the comments assume that the one who joins his ancestors will still be alive in some sense? Explain your answer.*

- *What, if anything, do these passages suggest about life beyond the grave?*

While the Bible's fullest teaching on life after death occurs in the New Testament, the Old Testament, including Genesis, indicates that the grave does not have the last word on human life.

The God of life would not allow death to cast the final and defining vote.

As far back as Genesis 5:24, Enoch does not even see death because "God took him to himself," thereby bringing Enoch into his presence forever alive. Much later when Abraham dies, the text says, "he joined his ancestors" (25:8). As Waltke explains, this phrase could not refer to Abraham's burial because he "was not buried with his ancestors. The same is true of Aaron (Num. 20:26) and Moses (Deut. 32:50)." Waltke then cites another Hebrew scholar who writes in his commentary on Genesis: "It would seem, therefore, that the existence of this idiom [which is unique to the Pentateuch], as of the corresponding figure to 'lie down with one's fathers,' testifies to a belief that, despite his mortality and perishability, man possesses an immortal element that survives the loss of life. Death is looked upon as a transition to an afterlife where one is united with one's ancestors."[68]

The book of Job, which many scholars believe to have been written during the time of patriarchs, records Job saying, "But as for me, I know that my Redeemer lives, and he will stand upon the earth at last. And after my body has decayed, yet in my body I will see God! I will see him for myself. Yes, I will see him with my own eyes. I am overwhelmed at the thought!" (Job 19:25–27 NLT). Much later, David writes in one of his psalms, "Even my body will rest confident and secure. For you [Yahweh] will not abandon me to the realm of death, nor will you allow your Faithful One to experience corruption" (Psalm 16:9–10). Centuries later, the apostle Peter would recognize David's words here as an affirmation of the king's bodily resurrection as well as of Jesus Christ's (Acts 2:24–31).

From Genesis to Revelation, life after death is affirmed and demonstrated to be true. We can rest in the knowledge that God has always held sway over death. His will be the last word, and his promise is that those who trust in him will live forever with him (John 3:14–16; Romans 5:12–21; 1 Corinthians 15:35–57; 2 Corinthians 5:1–10).

EXPERIENCE GOD'S HEART

- *Do you believe that, in Christ, you are already overcoming some of death's effects and that the grave will not hold you? If you are certain of this, note why. If you are not, review the passages cited in the "Digging Deeper" section and meditate on those. Ask the Holy Spirit to confirm within your spirit that you have everlasting life—even right now!—and that when you stop breathing, you won't stop living. One day, God will also raise your earthly body and transform it, fitting it for life everlasting in a new earth and new heaven (Revelation 20:11–22:5). You need not fear physical death. God has always overcome it.*

Reconciliation Confirmation and Joseph's Last Days

After the huge burial entourage returned to Egypt, Joseph's brothers grew anxious.

- *What were the brothers concerned over, and what did they do about it (Genesis 50:15–18)?*

- *How did Joseph address their anxiety (vv. 19–21)?*

- *Reflect on what Joseph told his brothers. What does it reveal about God's providence over human history? Does this comfort you? Explain your answer.*

♥ SHARE GOD'S HEART

Joseph shared God's heart with his brothers by fully forgiving them for the evil they had perpetuated against him. Joseph even shared with them how God worked their wickedness "for good... to ensure the survival of many people" (v. 20), a sovereign work that included the deliverance of the sinful brothers from starvation as well.

- *Is there someone in your life you need to forgive for what they have done to you? Share God's heart with them by forgiving them. Remember, forgiveness is not saying that what happened to you was okay in any sense. Rather, through forgiveness you are saying that you release the real wrong done to you, that you won't hold it against the person who hurt you. You may still not trust that person and have good reason not to. Still, by forgiving, you choose to let go of the wrong and move on with your life.[69]*

Genesis 50:22–26 tells us about Joseph's last days and finally his death.

- How old was Joseph when he died (vv. 22, 26)?

- *What did he get to see and do before he passed away (vv. 23–25)?*

- *What happened to his body after his death (v. 26)?*

 THE EXTRA MILE

There are numerous parallels between Joseph's life and Jesus'. To explore these, go to Appendix 3, "Pictures of Jesus in Joseph's Life." Read through the comparisons made there and note at least three that are particularly striking to you.

- *What insights into the lives of Jesus and Joseph did you glean from the comparisons you chose?*

- *What, if anything, do the comparisons tell you about the possibility of living Yahweh's way and the impact that can have in your life and that of others?*

Beyond Beginnings

The book of Genesis begins with the creation of life, including God's image bearers. It starts with great hope and expectations for a wondrous life on a plentiful, beautiful earth. God blesses his work and continues his engagement with it. He speaks to and walks with his first image bearers, sharing in their marital bliss in paradise.

The book ends with ongoing hope and expectations and some of God's image bearers still trusting in him. But now they experience death along with all other image bearers. The earth undergoes tremendous growth and devastating droughts. It has even been destroyed by floodwaters. Sin racks human life. Polygamy, idolatry, division, betrayal, deceit, rape, murder, war, slavery, and a host of other signs of corruption have become standard in a fallen, corrupted world. No one is exempt from sin's effects.

And yet...what God told Satan in Eden has been progressing too. The seed of Eve contains a chosen line—a line that, one day, will crush Satan's head. This line has come through Abel, Seth, Shem, Abraham, Isaac, and Israel. The fathers of the twelve tribes of Israel have been born. At the end of Genesis, the full story has not yet been told, but we're left with the knowledge that the God who creates, sustains, loves, blesses, judges, and reveals his will is going to keep bringing to pass what he has promised.

The rest of the Bible reveals the rest of the story, and it's filled with even more drama, miracles, blessings, judgments, hope, and fulfillment than the Book of Beginnings has shown. But what a great start is Genesis! And what a great God it reveals!

Talking It Out

1. The words of Israel and Joseph before their deaths reveal their confidence in the fulfillment of God's promises regarding the future possession of Canaan. Review what these men said in Genesis 48:21–22; 49:29–32; 50:24–25. Compare these passages to what Hebrews says about the patriarchs in 11:8–22. Do you possess this kind of confident faith in God? If not, why? What would it take for you to trust God this much? And if this is the kind of faith you have, what has helped produce it in your life?

2. Joseph told his fearful brothers, "Even though you intended to hurt me, God intended it for good. It was his plan all along, to ensure the survival of many people" (Genesis 50:20). Throughout Genesis, we have seen God bringing about good through and in spite of sinful people. What are some of the instances you recall revealed in Genesis? What have you learned about God and his ways through these accounts? Have they helped you rely on him more? If so, why?

3. In this study of Genesis, what are at least three truths or insights you have gained that have changed your understanding of God, his world, human beings, relationships, or you specifically? Share them with others and consider writing them down and placing them where you can revisit them and allow them to continue to influence you as time goes by.

Appendix

Pictures of Jesus in Joseph's Life

The life of Joseph gives us one of the clearest and most vivid pictures of the Lord Jesus Christ in the Bible. There is no one else in Scripture like Joseph, whose life points us to Jesus. It's like reading a preview of what Jesus would be like. There are so many fascinating parallels to Jesus embedded in the story line. Here are fifty comparisons between Joseph and Jesus Christ.

1. The meaning of Joseph's Hebrew name: Joseph means "adding" or "may he add." Adam was the great "subtractor," but Jesus, the last Adam, is the great "adder." Through the sacrifice made for every one of us, he gave us the opportunity to come in to his eternal family. Everyone who is saved is added to heaven's number. And the Father adds to the church daily those who are saved in Jesus' name. He added us to the body of believers at our salvation. And he adds dignity, purpose, and meaning to our lives. Joseph's name points us to Jesus and shows us that God not only added salvation to us but also added to us every spiritual blessing in Christ (Ephesians 1:3).

2. The meaning of Joseph's Egyptian names: Joseph had two names, the name his mother gave him and the name the Egyptians gave him. His Egyptian name was Zaphenath-Paneah, which means "revealer of secrets"

or possibly "God speaks through him and he (still) lives" (that is, God spoke through Joseph, and Joseph lived to tell about it!). Obviously, they gave Joseph that name because he was able to interpret Pharaoh's dreams and the dreams of his staff. Christ is the true "Revealer of Secrets" (Matthew 13:11), and God spoke through him, and he now lives forever in resurrection power. He is the revelator and the Great Revealer. Our Lord Jesus reveals what's going on in the hearts of men, and everything is revealed in his presence.

3. Joseph was a shepherd. Joseph fed his flock and cared for his father's sheep. And Jesus is the Great Shepherd of our lives (1 Peter 2:25), the Good Shepherd who guides (Psalm 23), and the Chief Shepherd, or Shepherd-King, who rewards (1 Peter 5:4).

4. Joseph was born to Jacob in his old age. Jesus was born on earth out of the eternity of the ages. From all eternity he was the Son of God. "In the very beginning the Living Expression was already there. And the Living Expression was with God, yet fully God" (John 1:1).

5. Jacob loved Joseph more than all his brothers. And so Father God loves his beautiful Son, Jesus. At his baptism, the Father's voice spoke, "This is the Son I love, and my greatest delight is in him" (Matthew 3:17).

6. Joseph wore a coat of many colors. This was a mark of honor and favor, and perhaps this multi-colored robe was a sign of the birthright. Jesus wore a seamless garment of righteousness. Revelation colors speak of Christ's virtues that surround him. Bright as the sun, glorious as the rainbow. Jesus has many colors, many virtues, many glories, and many perfections (Song of Songs 5:10–16).

7. The favor of Jacob and the rainbow-colored robe brought out the hatred of his brother's hearts toward young Joseph. Jesus likewise was hated because he exposed the wickedness of the hearts of men (John 3:19–20). Joseph's brothers wanted him dead, and so did Jesus' enemies. They wanted Jesus dead because he spoke the truth of God.

8. Joseph had a remarkable destiny. His dreams pointed him to the blessings that were yet to come. Each dream was a divine announcement of his exaltation. And Jesus as well had remarkable announcements made about him before he was even born. It was even prophesied that the responsibility of complete dominion would rest upon his shoulders (Isaiah 9:6–7). Both Joseph and Jesus had remarkable destinies.

9. Joseph dreamed of an earthly exaltation. One of Joseph's dreams was of his brothers bowing down to him, and that dream was fulfilled when they came to

buy food from him in Egypt. But this dream also points to the earthly reign that Jesus will one day experience. All his brothers (Jews) and gentiles will bow down to him and exalt his name (Philippians 2:9–10).

10. Another dream Joseph had involved the sun, moon, and stars bowing down to him. This pointed to the heavenly exaltation awaiting him. And Scripture says that Jesus was exalted above all his brothers and is now seated at the highest place (Ephesians 1:20–22). He is the Sovereign King, not only over the nations of the earth, but also over the kingdom of heaven. Both angels and the redeemed worship him (Revelation 4–5).

11. Joseph's brothers were envious of his dreams and the calling on his life. This caused his brothers to experience incredible jealousy. They couldn't stand to see their half-brother raised up over them. Jesus was anointed and favored by the Father. This infuriated the Pharisees so much that they finally crucified him out of envy (Matthew 27:17–18).

12. Joseph's father sent him to see how his brothers were, but they didn't want him there (Genesis 37:12–13). Jesus was also a sent one. He was sent from heaven as God's servant with a divine commission. He came to his own, but they wouldn't receive him either (John 1:11).

13. Joseph's father sent him to see about his brothers from the Valley of Hebron, and he was thrown in a pit and left for dead. *Hebron* means "fellowship." Jesus was sent from heaven, a place of perfect fellowship with the Father (John 1:18), to taste death for every man (Hebrews 2:9).

14. Joseph's brothers were at Shechem when he arrived to check on them. *Shechem* means "shoulder." The meaning of *shoulder* is a place that bears burdens. Jesus came to bear the burden of the Father and of humanity. He bowed his shoulders and became a servant to all (Philippians 2:6–7).

15. Joseph was found wandering in the fields looking for his brothers who didn't want him (Genesis 37:15–16). The fields are a picture of the world (Matthew 13:38). Our Lord Jesus walked through the fields of the earth seeking the lost and caring for the needy. He told his disciples that the foxes had holes and the birds had nests, but he had nowhere to rest (Matthew 8:20). He was looking for a resting place in the hearts of men but couldn't find it. Now his resting place is in the spirit of every believer (1 Corinthians 6:17).

16. Joseph found his brothers in Dothan. *Dothan* means "law" or "custom." And when Jesus found his people, they were all bound by the laws, customs, and traditions of their fathers (Acts 6:13–14).

17. Joseph's brothers hated him. And this jealous hatred caused them to plot. They wanted to take his life (Genesis 37:18). No sooner was Jesus born than the jealous hatred of him by the political powers of that day began to be displayed. Not only did Herod try to kill him, but the religious leaders of that day also discussed how they, too, might dispose of him (Matthew 12:14).

18. Joseph's words were not believed or valued by his brothers. They only hated him more for his words. They even ignored and despised his supernatural dreams. After Jesus was nailed to the cross, the people did not believe in him. They only reviled and mocked him, saying, "*If* you are the King" (Luke 23:37).

19. Joseph was stripped of his coat (Genesis 37:23). Jesus was stripped of his seamless garment (Matthew 27:27–28).

20. Joseph was cast into a pit. Jesus spent three days and three nights in the heart of the earth, or the pit of the earth (Matthew 12:40).

21. Joseph came out of the pit alive. Jesus came victorious out of his tomb taking captivity captive (Ephesians 4:8).

22. Joseph's brothers sold him into slavery with silver. Judas sold Jesus for silver. The Hebrew form of *Judas* is "Judah," the same name of the brother who sold Joseph.

23. Joseph's blood-sprinkled coat is shown to his father. Jesus' blood was taken within the veil before the Father (Hebrews 9:12). And his blood demonstrated to all of heaven that our sins were forgiven.

24. Joseph becomes a servant of others. He served Potiphar, and he served Pharaoh. Our heavenly Joseph, Jesus, came to earth not to be served but to serve. He came not to make a reputation but to give it all away in ministry for God and service to man (Philippians 2:5–12).

25. Joseph prospered, even as a servant (Genesis 39:2–3). Psalm 1 is a picture of the blessed man, Jesus, the One who prospers in everything he does. As a lowly, meek servant, Jesus prospered in all that he did.

26. Joseph's master was well pleased with him (Genesis 39:4). He walked in the fear of God and maintained his integrity in all things. So it was with Jesus. He could say, "I only do that which delights his (the Father's) heart" (John 8:29).

27. Joseph was tested severely yet did not sin (Genesis 39:7–12). And in Jesus, the devil could find no foothold in his personality (John 14:30). He was pure, undefiled, and separate from everything unclean (Hebrews 7:26). Demons and men tested him, but he proved to be blameless.

28. Joseph was falsely accused (Genesis 39:16–18). And false witnesses, who spoke against Jesus at his trial before the Sanhedrin, also made false accusations about him, our Lord and Savior (Mark 14:53–67).

29. Joseph did not defend himself when he was accused (Genesis 39:19). And when Jesus faced false accusations, the Scripture says that he didn't open his mouth but was silent through it all. He never spoke out in anger or self-defense (Isaiah 53:7).

30. Joseph was cast into prison (Genesis 39:20). And our Lord Jesus Christ was unjustly condemned by Herod, sentenced by the Roman authorities, and cast into prison (Matthew 27:1–30).

31. Joseph suffered greatly at the hands of the gentiles (Psalm 105:17–18). Jesus was treated unfairly as the rulers and authorities gathered together against him (Acts 4:26–27). He was mocked, spat upon, beaten, crowned with thorns, and nailed to the cross.

32. Joseph won the respect of the jailer (Genesis 39:21). As Jesus died, the Roman centurion testified that Jesus was a righteous man, the Son of God (Luke 23:47).

33. Joseph was imprisoned with two others (Genesis 40:1–3). Jesus was crucified between two thieves (Matthew 27:38), being numbered among the transgressors (Isaiah 53:12).

34. Joseph brought blessing to the one he was imprisoned with, the cupbearer, and pronounced judgment on the baker. Jesus took one thief into paradise with him, but the other thief mocked him and was left to die in his sins (Luke 23:39–42).

35. Yahweh revealed the future to Joseph through dreams. Jesus was the true prophet. He spoke from the Father's heart all that he was commanded to speak.

36. Joseph wanted to be remembered (Genesis 40:14). And the apostle Paul said the disciples were to remember Jesus as they gathered around the Lord's Table, as Christ had asked them to do (1 Corinthians 11:24).

37. Joseph was delivered out of his prison (Genesis 41:14). He was not destined to live out his days there. Instead he was lifted out of the place of shame and was given a seat of honor. And Jesus was laid in a

tomb temporarily (Acts 2:24), but he, too, was lifted up to the place of highest honor and rests at the right hand of God.

38. Joseph was recognized as a revealer of secrets. The butler, the baker, even Pharaoh benefited from the divine insight granted Joseph. Even the wise men in the land weren't able to interpret the dreams of Pharaoh. It was the Father of heaven that revealed the mysteries to Joseph and gave him insight to interpret dreams. Jesus Christ walked in the anointing of the Spirit of revelation and knew the thoughts of men's hearts. His eyes were always on the Father so that he understood the mysteries of heaven (John 8:28; 12:49).

39. Joseph was a wonderful counselor to Pharaoh. He not only interpreted dreams, but he also gave strategic wisdom to the world leader. Joseph walked out the manifest wisdom of God. Christ, too, has been given the title wonderful Counselor. God sent him to impart wisdom to the rulers of the earth and to instruct all of mankind on how to come to the Father and be prepared for their future (Isaiah 9:6–7; Psalm 2).

40. Joseph was exalted from shame to glory. And he shared the throne of Pharaoh while our Lord Jesus Christ shares the throne of Father God.

41. Joseph received a new name. And God has highly exalted Jesus Christ and given him a name that is above every other name, Jesus, the Savior of the world (Philippians 2:9–10; Matthew 1:21).

42. Joseph took a wife, a gentile, in a foreign country. So our Lord Jesus purchased his bride from the nations of the earth by his death on Calvary (Revelation 5:8–10).

43. Joseph's two sons were named Manasseh, which means "forgetting," and Ephraim, which means "fruitful." Their names remind us of the forgiveness of our sin and of the way our heavenly Father *forgets* all of our sin because of the work of the cross through Jesus Christ our Lord. And because of what he did for us, we share in the *fruitfulness* of his life in us as true sons and daughters (Galatians 5:22).

44. Joseph was thirty years old when he began his life's work (Genesis 41:46). And Jesus was thirty years old when he began his public ministry (Luke 3:23).

45. Joseph's season of exaltation resulted in a season of abundant blessing for his family and all who came from all over the world, hungry and needing food (Genesis 41:47–49). And in Jesus Christ, all who hunger can come to him and feast. He will feed them living Bread (John 6:51). Our heavenly Joseph gives

his bread to the hungry and perishing of this world so that they might experience the abundance of life found in Christ Jesus our Lord.

46. Joseph was unknown and unrecognized by his brothers (Genesis 42:8). For years they believed Joseph was dead and gone, not realizing that God had sent him ahead to prepare the way for their deliverance. So it is with our Lord Jesus. His brothers (Israel) do not know him, but he has gone into heaven and will soon receive them as they bow before their Messiah King (Philippians 2:9–11).

47. Joseph saw, recognized, and knew his brothers (Genesis 42:7). Even though they didn't recognize him, Joseph's eyes were upon them. So the eyes of the Lord Jesus have been upon the Jews all through the long night of their rejection (Jeremiah 16:17; Hosea 5:3).

48. Joseph revealed himself to his brothers the second time they saw him. Stephen emphasized this in his parting message to Israel (Acts 7:13). The first time the brothers saw Joseph, they did not recognize him, but on their second visit to Egypt, Joseph revealed himself to them. The first time the Lord Jesus was seen by his brethren after the flesh, they knew him not, but when they see him the second time, he shall be known by them, and they will accept him as their Messiah (Revelation 1:7–8).

49. Joseph demonstrated tremendous grace toward his brothers. Joseph graciously wanted his brothers to come close to him, and then he kissed each one. He even encouraged them not to be grieved over what they had done or angry with themselves (Genesis 45:4–5, 15). So shall it be when Israel is reconciled to Christ (Isaiah 54:7–8; Zechariah 13:1).

50. Joseph was a man of compassion and deep feelings. Seven times he wept. He wept when he listened to his brothers confessing their guilt (Genesis 42:24). He wept when he first saw Benjamin (43:30). He wept when he revealed his identity to his brothers (45:12). He wept as he reconciled with his brothers (45:15). He wept when he saw his father Jacob (46:29). He wept at the death of his father (50:1). And he wept when his brothers questioned his love for them (50:15–17). Jesus Christ was also tenderhearted and was often moved with compassion. We are told Jesus wept at least twice, once at the graveside of Lazarus (Luke 11:22) and later over Jerusalem (Luke 19:41–44).

Endnotes

1 "About The Passion Translation," *The Passion Translation: The New Testament with Psalms, Proverbs, and Song of Songs* (Savage, MN: BroadStreet Publishing Group, 2017), iv.

2 The *toledot* formula and the family histories they record are explained in *TPT: The Book of Genesis – Part 1* (Savage, MN: BroadStreet Publishing Group, 2021), Lesson 1, under the heading "Literary Type."

3 Merrill Unger, "Patriarchal Age, The," *The New Unger's Bible Dictionary*, ed. R. K. Harrison (Chicago: Moody Press, 1988), 967. Hebrew scholar J. Barton Payne dates Abraham and the patriarchal period close to Unger's dates, with just a few years difference. See J. Barton Payne, *An Outline of Hebrew History* (Grand Rapids, MI: Baker Book House, 1954), 34–36.

4 Benjamin C. Chapman, "Ur," *The New International Dictionary of Biblical Archaeology*, ed. E. M. Blaiklock and R. K. Harrison (Grand Rapids, MI: Zondervan, 1983), 462.

5 Unger, "Ur of the Chaldees," *The New Unger's Bible Dictionary*, 1321.

6 Gleason L. Archer Jr., *A Survey of Old Testament Introduction*, revised ed. (Chicago: Moody Press, 2007), 142.

7 Unger, "Ur of the Chaldees," *The New Unger's Bible Dictionary*, 1321.

8 Archer, *A Survey of Old Testament Introduction*, 182.

9 Archer, *A Survey of Old Testament Introduction*, 183; see also Unger, "Ur of the Chaldees," *The New Unger's Bible Dictionary*, 1321.

10 Brian Simmons, "Introduction" to Genesis, *The Passion Translation* (Savage, MN: BroadStreet Publishing Group, 2020), 3.

11 W. E. Vine, Merrill F. Unger, and William White Jr., "To Bless," *An*

Expository Dictionary of Biblical Words (Nashville, TN: Thomas Nelson, 1985), 18.

12 Unger, "Haran, City of," *The New Unger's Bible Dictionary*, 535.

13 Payne, *An Outline of Hebrew History*, 39.

14 Allen P. Ross, "Genesis," *The Bible Knowledge Commentary: Old Testament*, ed. John F. Walvoord and Roy B. Zuck (Wheaton, IL: Victor Books, 1985), 50.

15 The biblical view of salvation is comprehensive. We are saved from the *penalty* of sin (justification), the *power* of sin (sanctification), and eventually from the very *presence* of sin (glorification). *Justification* gives us a righteous standing before God; we are guiltless, without condemnation, before our divine Judge (Romans 5:1; 8:1). It is "the act by which God gets us out of sin (legally)." *Sanctification*, however, is the process "by which God gets sin out of us (actually)." The Spirit works in us to make us righteous in what we think, feel, and do (Romans 6; 8). And glorification is the future act that delivers us into a world free of sin, death, and Satan and finishes transforming us so we can live forever as the image bearers we were always created to be (Romans 8:18–23; Revelation 21). In other words, salvation is a three-step process that leads to our complete liberation from sin and its dire consequences. (Quotations are from Norman L. Geisler, *Systematic Theology, Volume 3: Sin, Salvation* [Bloomington, MN: Bethany House, 2004], 237.)

16 Bruce K. Waltke with Cathi J. Fredricks, *Genesis: A Commentary* (Grand Rapids, MI: Zondervan Academic, 2001), 225.

17 Waltke, *Genesis*, 228.

18 Waltke, *Genesis*, 232.

19 Genesis 14:18, note 'e,' TPT.

20 Don Richardson, *Eternity in Their Hearts* (Ventura, CA: Regal Books, 1981), 7.

21 Richardson, *Eternity in Their Hearts*, 8.

22 Gordon J. Wenham, *Genesis 1–15, Volume 1*, Word Biblical Commentary series, gen. ed. David A. Hubbard and Glenn W. Barker (Grand Rapids, MI: Zondervan, 1987), 327.

23 For an excellent discussion of covenants in Scripture, see "Covenant (in the New Testament)" and "Covenant (in the Old Testament)," both by J. Barton Payne, *The Zondervan Pictorial Encyclopedia of the Bible*, ed. Merrill C. Tenney (Grand Rapids, MI: Zondervan, 1976), vol. 1, 995–1010.

24 Wenham, *Genesis 1–15*, 333.

25 Gordon J. Wenham, *Genesis 16–50, Volume 2*, Word Biblical Commentary series, gen. ed. David A. Hubbard and Glenn W. Barker (Grand Rapids, MI: Zondervan, 2000), 7.

26 Wenham, *Genesis 16–50*, 9.

27 Wenham, *Genesis 16–50*, 9.

28 Norman L. Geisler, *Systematic Theology: Volume Two: God, Creation* (Minneapolis, MN: Bethany House, 2003), 600, emphasis in the original. See also Geisler's book *To Understand the Bible Look for Jesus*, reprint ed. (Grand Rapids, MI: Baker Book House, 1979), 50–51; and C. Fred Dickason, *Angels: Elect and Evil* (Chicago: Moody Press, 1975), ch. 6.

29 Ross, "Genesis," *The Bible Knowledge Commentary*, 59.

30 Waltke, *Genesis*, 282.

31 For much more on the Moabites and Ammonites and their role in biblical history, see Unger, "Moabite, Moabites," 879–81; "Ammonites," 53, *The New Unger's Bible Dictionary*.

32 Genesis 20:1, note 'e,' TPT.

33 Waltke, *Genesis*, 303.

34 If you would like to explore how the disciples imitated Jesus and how we can learn from their example, see Michael Griffiths, *The Example of Jesus* (Downers Grove, IL: InterVarsity Press, 1985).

35 Waltke, *Genesis*, 313.

36 Wenham, *Genesis 16–50*, 119–20.

37 Wenham, *Genesis 16–50*, 130.

38 Genesis 24:61, note 'c,' TPT.

39 Wenham, *Genesis 16–50*, 158; see also Genesis 25:1, note 'c,' TPT.

40 Waltke, *Genesis*, 338.

41 Waltke, *Genesis*, 347.

42 Ross, "Genesis," *The Bible Knowledge Commentary*, 71.

43 Wenham, *Genesis 16–50*, 205.

44 Waltke, *Genesis*, 381.

45 Wenham, *Genesis 16–50*, 249.

46 Waltke, *Genesis*, 415.

47 Ross, "Genesis," *The Bible Knowledge Commentary*, 77.

48 Genesis 33:18, note 'd,' TPT.

49 Waltke, *Genesis*, 465.

50 Waltke, *Genesis*, 481.

51 Unger, "Esau," *The New Unger's Bible Dictionary*, 373.

52 See Ross, "Genesis," *The Bible Knowledge Commentary*, 85; Wenham, *Genesis 16–50*, 336.

53 Payne, *An Outline of Hebrew History*, 46.

54 Wenham, *Genesis 16–50*, 350.

55 Waltke, *Genesis*, 502.

56 Unger, "Judah," *The New Unger's Bible Dictionary*, 719.

57 Derek Kidner, *Genesis: An Introduction and Commentary*, Tyndale Old Testament Commentaries, ed. D. J. Wiseman (Downers Grove, IL: InterVaristy Press, 1967), 187.

58 Wenham, *Genesis 16–50*, 365.

59 Payne, *An Outline of Hebrew History*, 46.

60 Genesis 40:1, note 'b,' TPT.

61 Wenham, *Genesis 16–50*, 357.

62 Genesis 41:45, note 'f,' TPT.

63 Waltke, *Genesis*, 534.

64 Payne, *An Outline of Hebrew History*, 47.

65 Joshua J. Mark, "Middle Kingdom of Egypt," *World History Encyclopedia*, October 4, 2016, https://www.ancient.eu/Middle_Kingdom_of_Egypt.

66 Waltke, *Genesis*, 560.

67 Wenham, *Genesis 16–50*, 442.

68 Waltke, *Genesis*, 340–41.

69 For an excellent discussion of forgiveness, see Lewis B. Smedes, *Forgive and Forget: Healing the Hurts We Don't Deserve*, 2nd ed. (San Francisco, CA: HarperOne, 2007).